Kingfisher
Science
Encyclopedia

General Editor: Catherine Headlam

2

BOND, CHEMICAL ● CORROSION

Kingfisher

KINGFISHER
an imprint of Larousse plc
Elsley House, 24–30 Great Titchfield Street
London W1P 7AD

First published by Kingfisher 1991
Reprinted 1993, 1995 (with revisions) (twice), 1997

British Library Cataloguing-in-Publication Data
A catalogue record for this book is available from the British Library

ISBN 0 85697 448 0

Typesetting: Tradespools Ltd, Frome,
Somerset
Printed in Spain

GENERAL EDITOR
Catherine Headlam

EDITORIAL DIRECTOR
Jim Miles

ASSISTANT EDITORS
Lee Simmons
Charlotte Evans

EDITORIAL ASSISTANT
Andrea Moran

CONSULTANTS
Professor Lawrence F. Lowery, University of California, Berkeley, USA
Alison Porter, Education Officer, Science Museum, London

EDUCATIONAL CONSULTANTS
Terry Cash, Coordinator of a team of advisory teachers in Essex
Robert Pressling, Maths Coordinator,
Hillsgrove Primary School, London

CONTRIBUTORS
Joan Angelbeck
Michael Chinery
John Clark
Neil Curtis
Gwen Edmonds
Andrew Fisher
William Gould
Ian Graham
William Hemsley
James Muirden
John Paton
Brian Ward
Wendy Wasels
Peter Way

DESIGN
Ralph Pitchford
Allan Hardcastle
Ross George
Judy Crammond

PICTURE RESEARCH
Tim Russell
Elaine Willis

PRODUCTION
Dawn Hickman

SAFETY CODE

Some science experiments can be dangerous. Ask an adult to help you with difficult hammering or cutting and any experiments that involve flames, hot liquids or chemicals. Do not forget to put out any flames and turn off the heat when you have finished. Good scientists avoid accidents.

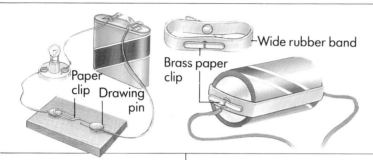

Paper clip

Drawing pin

Brass paper clip

Wide rubber band

ELECTRICITY
- Never use mains electricity for experiments.
- Use batteries for all experiments that need electricity. Dispose of batteries carefully when they are used up and never heat them up or take them apart.

HEATING
- Tie back hair and be careful of loose clothes.
- Only heat small quantities of a substance.
- Always have an adult with you.
- Never heat any container with a top on it. Always point what you are heating away from you.
- Never hold something in your hands to heat it. Use a holder that does not conduct heat.

SAFE SOURCES OF HEAT
- Hot water from the tap or kettle is a good source of heat.
- A hair dryer can be used to dry things. Always take care when using electricity near water.

- For direct heat use a night light or short thick candle placed in sand in a metal tray.

Sand

Metal tray

CHEMICALS AND QUANTITIES
- Only use a small amount of any substance even if it is just salt or vinegar.
- Never taste or eat chemicals
- Clean up all spillages immediately, especially if on your skin.
- Wash your hands after using chemicals.
- Always ask an adult before using any substance; many cooking or cleaning substances used at home are quite powerful.
- Smell chemicals very carefully. Do not breathe in deeply any strong smells.
- Never handle chemicals with your bare hands. Use an old spoon and wash it very carefully after use.
- Label **all** chemicals.

SUN
- Never look directly at the Sun, especially when using a telescope or binoculars.

PLANTS AND ANIMALS
- Never pick wild flowers.
- Collect insects carefully so as not to harm them. Release them afterwards.
- Be careful of stinging insects.

SAFE CONTAINERS
- Use plastic containers if an experiment does not require heating or strong chemicals.
- Use heat-proof glass or metal containers if you are using heat.
- Avoid using ordinary glass as it may shatter.

CUTTING
- Use scissors rather than a knife whenever possible.
- When using a knife keep your fingers behind the cutting edge.
- Put what you are cutting on a board that will not slip and will prevent damage to the surface underneath.

Bond, chemical

Chemical bonds hold together the ATOMS in COMPOUNDS. There are two main types: *ionic bonds* and *covalent bonds*. An atom is made up of a postively-charged nucleus and negatively-charged ELECTRONS which circle round it. Ionic bonds are formed when electrons are transferred between certain atoms so that the atoms become IONS. In sodium chloride (common salt), for example, a sodium atom gives up one of its electrons to become a positive ion. The electron is passed to a chlorine atom, which becomes a negative ion. Ions of opposite charges attract each other so the positive sodium ion and the negative chloride ion bond together and form sodium chloride. In covalent bonding, two or more atoms, for example hydrogen and oxygen atoms, join by sharing pairs of electrons.

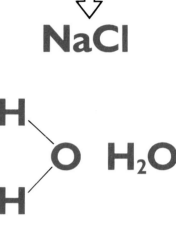

▲ *In ionic bonding (top) one atom takes an electron from another atom. In covalent bonding, electrons are shared.*

Bone

Bone is the very hard, living material that makes up the SKELETONS of most vertebrates. There are 206 bones in the adult human body. Some are very tiny. The largest is the femur, which runs from the hip to the knee. Bones contain tiny living CELLS, which is why bones can mend themselves. The cells produce a tough PROTEIN called collagen which gives the bones their strength. They also secrete calcium and phosphorus salts which give the bones their hardness. Not all the skeleton is bone, some parts are made of *cartilage* (gristle). It is not as hard as bone because it does not contain calcium salts. The skeletons of some primitive fish, such as sharks, are made entirely of cartilage.

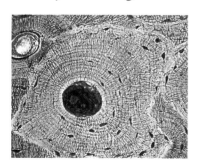

◄ *The skeleton which supports humans is made up of two kinds of bones: the long bones, which are mainly in the arms and the legs, and the short bones in, for example, the skull and the spine. This bone cell is part of the compact bone tissue forming the solid, outer part of the femur or thigh bone.*

Linus Pauling (1901–)
A United States chemist, Linus Pauling won the 1954 Nobel Prize for Chemistry for his work on chemical bonding. He calculated the energies needed to bind atoms in a molecule, the distances between the atoms and the angles at which bonds form. Also he won the Nobel Prize for Peace in 1962.

Botany

Botany is the study of plants. *See* pages 78 and 79.

BOTANY

Botany is a very important branch of biology covering the study of plants. Only plants can manufacture food from simple materials using the energy of the Sun, so every food chain begins with a plant, and every animal on Earth, including people, depends on plant-life for its food. Plants also recycle the air that we breathe, absorbing much of the carbon dioxide and giving out the oxygen that we need. We get many of our clothes and medicines from plants; trees provide timber which is needed for houses, furniture and making paper. Much of the world's population relies on wood for fuel, for warmth and cooking.

The Greeks began the serious study of plants over 2000 years ago, but it was not until microscopes were invented that people really began to learn how plants are constructed. Today more powerful microscopes and advances in biochemistry have enabled us to discover more about what goes on inside plants. It was only in the 18th century that a Swedish naturalist called Linnaeus started to name plants systematically. Now we know that there are over 300,000 species of plants in the world. Not surprisingly, botany is divided into many branches, and botanists usually specialize in one branch or another. Many work in agriculture and horticulture, helping us to grow better crops.

▲ Many plants produce spores (top) which can develop into new plants. In ferns (bottom), the spores are held under the leaves.

SEE FOR YOURSELF
Draw pictures of several plants. Carefully copy the shape of flower petals and leaves. Write the name of the plant and where you found it by each drawing. You can find most of the names of plants in a field guide or other plant book. See if you can label the parts of the flowers. Look under FLOWER in this encyclopedia if you need help with this.

small flower   short fruit

stalked

▼ Spirogyra and Sea lettuce are both green algae, though Spirogyra is found in ponds and Sea lettuce is a seaweed. Bladder wrack, also a seaweed, is a brown alga.

▼ Mosses, such as Bryum capillare, and ferns are two major groups of plants.

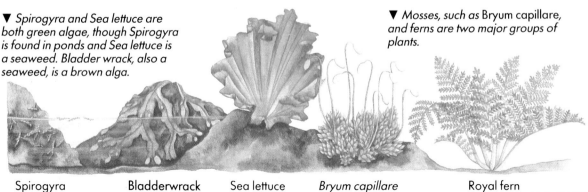

Spirogyra   Bladderwrack   Sea lettuce   *Bryum capillare*   Royal fern

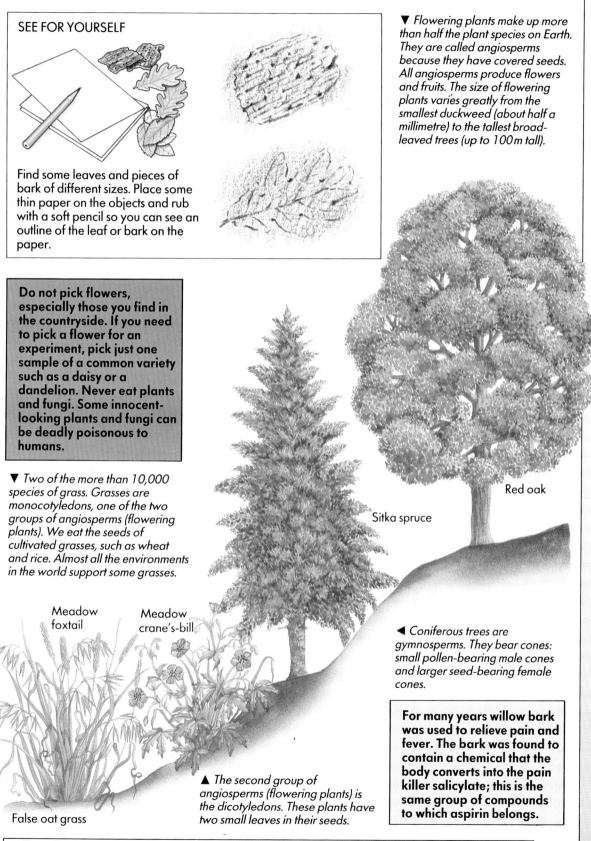

Find some leaves and pieces of bark of different sizes. Place some thin paper on the objects and rub with a soft pencil so you can see an outline of the leaf or bark on the paper.

Do not pick flowers, especially those you find in the countryside. If you need to pick a flower for an experiment, pick just one sample of a common variety such as a daisy or a dandelion. Never eat plants and fungi. Some innocent-looking plants and fungi can be deadly poisonous to humans.

▼ Two of the more than 10,000 species of grass. Grasses are monocotyledons, one of the two groups of angiosperms (flowering plants). We eat the seeds of cultivated grasses, such as wheat and rice. Almost all the environments in the world support some grasses.

▼ Flowering plants make up more than half the plant species on Earth. They are called angiosperms because they have covered seeds. All angiosperms produce flowers and fruits. The size of flowering plants varies greatly from the smallest duckweed (about half a millimetre) to the tallest broad-leaved trees (up to 100 m tall).

Red oak

Sitka spruce

Meadow foxtail

Meadow crane's-bill

◀ Coniferous trees are gymnosperms. They bear cones: small pollen-bearing male cones and larger seed-bearing female cones.

For many years willow bark was used to relieve pain and fever. The bark was found to contain a chemical that the body converts into the pain killer salicylate; this is the same group of compounds to which aspirin belongs.

False oat grass

▲ The second group of angiosperms (flowering plants) is the dicotyledons. These plants have two small leaves in their seeds.

See also AGRICULTURE; BIOLOGY; CHLOROPHYLL; COTYLEDON; CYTOLOGY; HORTICULTURE; LEAVES; MICROSCOPE; ORGANISM; SPECIES; ZOOLOGY.

▲ *Tycho Brahe, the astronomer who observed the planets.*

The brain contains more than 10 billion neurons with complex pathways linking our senses, our movements, and memory. The signals transmitted through these routes enable us to eat, walk, lift loads, speak, make decisions, and so on.

Cod

Olfactory bulb   Optic lobe

Frog

Horse

▲ *The brains of lesser-evolved animals have clearer functional divisions than the human brain. The olfactory bulb is associated with smell, and the optic lobe with sight.*

▶ *The largest area of the human brain is the cerebrum, which controls conscious feeling and voluntary movements. (Right) Different areas of the cerebrum control the various different functions.*

Boyle, Robert *See* Chemistry

Brahe, Tycho

Tycho Brahe (1546–1601), a Danish astronomer, lived before the TELESCOPE was invented and made the most accurate observations with the naked eye ever known. Like most astronomers of the time, he was employed by his king as an astrologer who had to cast horoscopes, but his real interest was the movement of the PLANETS. He believed that the planets orbit the Sun, but he also thought that the Sun orbits the Earth and that our planet was the center of the UNIVERSE. Brahe set out to prove this by observing the positions of the planets.

After his death the observations reached the hands of Johannes KEPLER, who was studying the same problem. Brahe's naked eye observations helped Kepler prove that the Earth also revolves around the Sun, and that the planets move in ellipses, not circles.

Brain

The brain is the largest and most important part of an animal's nervous system. In vertebrates, the brain is held in place and protected by the skull. The brains of invertebrates are generally much simpler and are often no more than swellings of NERVES at the head end.

The brain's function is to control the body. It uses

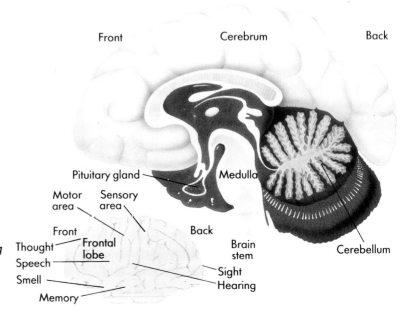

Front   Cerebrum   Back

Pituitary gland   Medulla

Motor   Sensory
area   area

Front   Back
Thought Frontal   Brain
Speech   lobe   stem   Cerebellum
Smell   Sight
                          Hearing
Memory

information from sense organs such as the EYES and the EARS. It then decides what action is needed and sends messages through the nerves to the MUSCLES or GLANDS. The brain can also store information for use at a later date. In other words, it can learn and remember things. Most animals can learn, but humans are better at learning because their brains are relatively larger than those of other animals. Our brains have also developed language for communication and for expressing ideas.
See also INSTINCT; LEARNING; SENSES.

Neuron A nerve cell in the nervous system.
Cerebellum This controls muscles and balance.
Medulla This controls involuntary activities such as breathing.
Cerebral hemisphere The cerebrum is divided into left and right hemispheres connected in the middle by bundles of nerve fibres.

Brass *See* Alloy

Breathing

All animals need OXYGEN to burn up food and produce ENERGY in their bodies. This is called respiration, and the process of getting the oxygen into the body is called breathing. Land-living vertebrates breathe with LUNGS, which are filled with air and then emptied again by

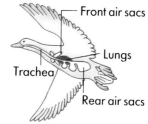

▲ *Birds breathe using a system of air sacs as well as lungs.*

◄ *Breathing in humans is assisted by the diaphragm. It contracts (moves down) when we breathe in, and is relaxed when we breathe out.*

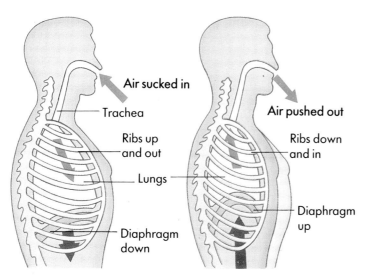

SEE FOR YOURSELF
Push a balloon through the top of a plastic bottle. Tape the balloon's mouth tightly around the neck of the bottle. Cut the end off the bottle and tape a piece of balloon over the bottom. Pull the rubber down to give the effect of the diaphragm contracting. The pressure in the bottle falls and the balloon is filled with air.

muscular movements of the chest and throat. In the lungs, the oxygen from the air passes into the animal's BLOOD and is then carried around the body. Fishes breathe with GILLS which take oxygen from water that has been sucked in through the mouth. Insects breathe through tiny holes called spiracles that are found in a line on each side of the body. The air is carried right into the insect's body by a network of slender tubes. Active insects like wasps often also use bellow-like movements of their bodies to pump the air along.

Bos primigenius
Ancestor of modern cattle

Aberdeen Angus
Domestic descendant

▲ *Modern cattle have been bred so that they produce more meat and less fat.*

▶ *Breeders have developed varieties of strawberry plants that can produce large, juicy, disease-resistant fruit throughout the summer and autumn months.*

▼ *Shafts of sunlight show up the particles of dust and smoke in the air. Particles are struck by fast-moving, invisible molecules of gases in the air, which cause them to move about at random. This is called Brownian motion.*

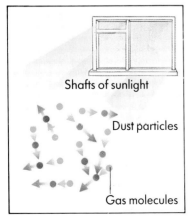

Shafts of sunlight

Dust particles

Gas molecules

Breeding

Breeding means producing offspring. People have controlled the REPRODUCTION of plants and animals so that they develop features that we consider useful. A Jersey cow, for example, can produce at least 40 litres of milk every day, but a wild cow can produce only about 4 litres of milk in a day (enough to feed its calf). Jersey cows give so much milk because dairy farmers in the past have carefully picked out those cows that gave the most milk, and allowed only these cows to mate and produce calves. By repeating this process year after year, the farmers eventually produced the Jersey breed. By selecting only animals or plants with particular features, people have bred hundreds of horses, garden flowers and crops, and can produce varieties of plants that are resistant to various diseases.

Cultivated strawberry plant

Wild strawberry plant

Bridges *See* Construction

Bronze *See* Alloy

Brownian motion

Brownian motion is the continual random movement of microscopic particles suspended in a LIQUID or GAS. The particles move as if being hit by the fluid. In fact, that is just what is happening. Molecules in the fluid constantly move around and bump into the particles causing them to move. The hotter the fluid is, the faster the particles vibrate because the molecules are moving faster too. The movement is in any direction, and this is why particles of a material will, in time, spread evenly throughout a fluid. Dust, smoke and smells spread through air in this way. Brownian motion was discovered by Robert Brown (1773–1858), a Scottish botanist and physicist, while studying the motion of pollen grains in water in 1827. Brownian motion was seen as positive evidence of the existence of ATOMS and MOLECULES.

Bubbles

A bubble is a spherical region of GAS, such as AIR, found inside a liquid or surrounded by a thin film of liquid. Water with detergent in it forms thin films well because the detergent molecules tend to line themselves up with one end pointing in and the other, out, making the surface of the liquid more stable. Soap bubbles are shaped by the balance between the outward PRESSURE of the gas inside and the inward force of SURFACE TENSION which tends to make the surface shrink. The thickness of the liquid layer is due to the detergent molecules and is the same for bubbles of different sizes; COLOURS can be seen because of the DIFFRACTION of light through the layer.

SEE FOR YOURSELF
Mix 1 egg cup full of washing-up liquid with 3 egg-cups-full of water. Make different sized bubble frames out of thin wire. Dip a frame into the solution and blow through it gently.

◀ Diffraction of light on the surface of a bubble makes coloured patterns.

Bunsen burner

The bunsen burner produces a flame by burning NATURAL GAS from a small metal pipe. The TEMPERATURE and intensity of the flame can be adjusted by controlling the air supply. Since its invention in 1850 by the German scientist Robert Wilhelm Bunsen (1811–1899), it has provided an instant and efficient source of heat for scientific experiments. It is a familiar item in laboratories around the world.

See also BURNING; COMBUSTION; INSTRUMENTS, SCIENTIFIC.

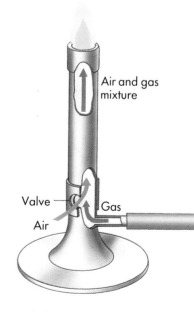

Air and gas mixture

Valve

Gas

Air

▲ With the air valve open, the gas flowing through a bunsen burner burns completely and produces a flame that is very hot, about 1500°C.

Buoyancy

Buoyancy is the name given to the upward FORCES exerted on an object when it is in a liquid or gas (a fluid). These forces appear because the PRESSURE in a fluid increases with depth, so that the upward pressure exerted on the bottom of the object is greater than the downward pressure exerted on the top.

If the upward buoyancy forces are greater than the downward force of GRAVITY, the object floats in the fluid. The buoyancy forces behave as one force applied at a point called the centre of buoyancy; the body will float stably with the centre of buoyancy above the CENTRE OF GRAVITY. Ships have to be carefully designed so that the centre of gravity remains below the centre of buoyancy even when they are rolling in heavy seas.
See also ARCHIMEDES; FLOTATION.

▼ *In laboratories technicians test different materials to find the temperatures that the materials must be heated to before they burst into flames and burn.*

Burning

Burning is the common word for what chemists call COMBUSTION. It is a process in which a substance combines very rapidly with a gas, producing heat and light. The light usually appears in the form of a flame. The gas most often involved in burning is OXYGEN, but reactions involving other gases are also examples of burning. Controlled burning of FUEL containing HYDROCARBONS such as oil, coal and natural gas helps to produce energy for heating and the production of ELECTRICITY.
See also ENERGY; OXIDATION AND REDUCTION.

Butane *See* Propane

Cable television *See* Television

Caffeine

Caffeine is a chemical COMPOUND of carbon, nitrogen, hydrogen and oxygen. It is an odourless, crystalline SOLID, slightly bitter to the taste and is SOLUBLE in water and alcohol. Caffeine occurs naturally in small amounts in tea, coffee, cacao (chocolate tree) and cola nuts but can also be made artificially. Caffeine speeds up the blood CIRCULATION and the working of the nervous system. In small doses, it is not thought to have ill-effects, but when taken in excess it can cause nervousness, loss of sleep, headaches and digestive trouble.

Cola drinks contain caffeine (about 2 percent) from the cola nut, a nut from the tropical cola tree. In South America and Africa the nuts are chewed to fight tiredness. An average cup of coffee contains about 150 mg of caffeine, a harmless amount on its own but too much if you drink 10 or more cups a day.

Calcium

Calcium is a softish, silvery-white metallic ELEMENT that reacts readily with water or oxygen. It makes up 3.6 percent of the Earth's crust and is found in nature as COMPOUNDS. Calcium carbonate forms limestone, CHALK and marble. Calcium sulphate occurs as gypsum. Pure calcium, used in certain ALLOYS, is obtained by passing an electric current through molten calcium chloride. Calcium and its compounds have many industrial uses. Among the most important compounds are calcium oxide (lime); calcium chloride; calcium fluoride and calcium sulphate (used in CEMENT and plaster). Calcium compounds, present in green vegetables and milk, are essential for strong bones and teeth.

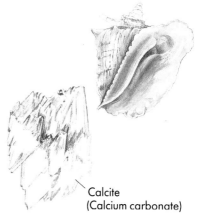

Seashell
(Calcium carbonate)

Calcite
(Calcium carbonate)

▲ The mineral calcium carbonate forms the shells of molluscs and other sea animals, as well as the pearls of oysters and eggshells. It also makes up 4–6 percent of the Moon.

◀ Under an electron microscope calcium sulphate crystals appear as needle-like structures. They form part of the 'fur' found on the inside of kettles in hard-water areas.

The first true electronic calculator was produced in Britain by the Bell Punch Company in 1963. It had a display 20 cm wide, which is as wide as this book. It could perform only 4 functions: addition, subtraction, multiplication and division.

Calculator

A calculator is an electronic device used for calculations. It consists of a set of numbered keys and a display that shows which keys have been pressed as well as the answers to the calculations. Inside the calculator is an INTEGRATED CIRCUIT that can perform calculations much more quickly than a person. Some calculators are almost as small and thin as credit cards. The simplest calculators can carry out simple ARITHMETIC functions (addition, subtraction, multiplication and division). More advanced calculators can perform other functions. Some can be programmed like a COMPUTER. The first electronic calculators were sold in 1971. Most of them were made in Japan. In 1974, the British company Hewlett-Packard introduced the first programmable calculator. It could be programmed to solve mathematical problems.

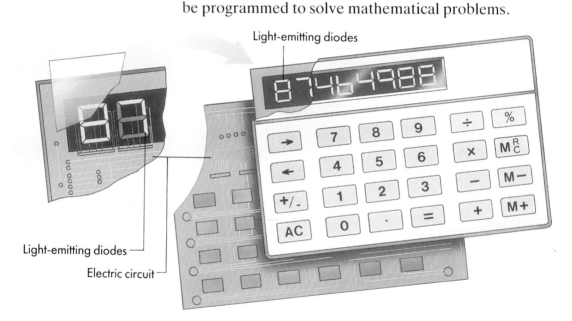

Light-emitting diodes

Light-emitting diodes

Electric circuit

▲ Most modern pocket calculators use silicon chips and have a light-emitting diode display. This calculator can add, subtract, multiply and divide as fast as we can press the keys. More advanced calculators can also do more difficult scientific calculations.

Calendar

Calendars are used to measure and record the passage of TIME. For thousands of years most calendars were based on either the observation of the phases of the MOON or the Earth's orbit round the Sun. Julius Caesar introduced the Julian calendar in 46 BC, which is the basis of the one we use today. It had a 365-day year, with one extra day added every fourth, or leap, year because the solar year, the time the Earth takes to go round the Sun is about 365$\frac{1}{4}$ days. This was inaccurate because the calendar year was about 11 minutes longer than the solar year. The difference soon became noticeable, reaching 10 days in 1582. Pope Gregory dropped the extra 10 days in that year, instructing that 5 October should become 15 October. He said leap years should not happen on centenary years except for multiples of 400, which is why the year 2000, unlike 1900 and 1800, will be a leap year.

◀ *The 20 days in the Aztec month are represented in the inner ring of this calendar stone.*

A 13-month year is one of the proposals for the reform of the present calendar. Each month would be exactly 4 weeks long. An extra month called Sol would be placed between June and July. A 'Year Day' at the end of the year would not belong to a week or month, and every 4 years a 'Leap-Year Day' would be added before 1 July.

Calorie *See* Joule

Camcorder *See* Video camera

Camera

A camera is a device for taking photographs. It has an opening called an aperture in one side to let light in and light-sensitive FILM on the opposite side to register the image. A LENS in front of the aperture focuses the light into a sharp image on the film. The earliest cameras made in the 19th century were large and heavy. They were called plate cameras because they used copper or, more commonly, glass plates coated with chemicals to register the image. A photograph was taken by removing the lens cap to let light enter the camera for perhaps 30 seconds and then replacing the cap. People had to stay still for a long time to have their photographs taken.

Most modern cameras use rolls of film instead of plates, but disc cameras use discs of film. Film is usually taken out of the camera and developed with chemicals to

SEE FOR YOURSELF
Paint the inside of a box and its lid black. Cut out a square from the side and stick tracing paper or photographic paper over the opening, the 'screen'. Make a small hole, the 'viewer', in the opposite side of the box. Point the 'viewer' at a well lit object.

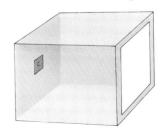

An upside-down image of the object appears on the screen. Light rays from the object travel in straight lines and cross as they pass through the hole.

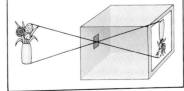

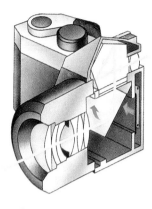

▲ *When a photograph is being taken by an SLR camera, seen here in cross section, the mirror lifts up, the shutter opens to expose the film and closes again. The light makes an upside-down picture of the image on the film. The film is wound on and later developed and made into negatives from which prints are made.*

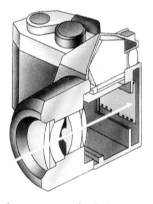

▲ *In a camera the light passes through the lens, then through the diaphragm, which is adjusted to let in the correct amount of light.*

SLR cameras with automatic shutter releases and automatic film winders can take several pictures every second. The fastest camera in the world, used in scientific research at London's Imperial College of Science and Technology, can process 33,000 million images every second.

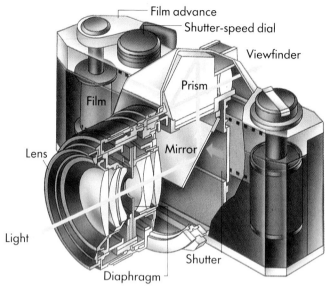

▲ *In a Single Lens Reflex (SLR) camera there is a mirror which reflects the image seen through the lens up to the viewfinder.*

reveal the images on it. The exception is the instant picture camera, for example a POLAROID CAMERA, which produces photographs that develop by themselves. All but the simplest cameras allow the photographer to control the amount of light that enters the camera by changing the size of the aperture and the length of time that the shutter is open (the shutter speed).

A very popular type of camera is the Single Lens Reflex (SLR). Light entering the lens of an SLR camera is reflected by a mirror up to the top of the camera where it is reflected again to emerge through the eyepiece. This enables the photographer to see the same image that will form the picture on the film. Other cameras have a separate lens and viewfinder.

See also DAGUERREOTYPE; FOCUS; PHOTOGRAPHY.

Camouflage

Camouflage is an ADAPTATION of many animals that makes them difficult to be seen. Some animals hide from their enemies and others from their prey. Camouflage usually involves colours and special shapes, which help the animals to blend in with their backgrounds so that they are not noticed. Many caterpillars are green and very difficult to see when they are sitting on leaves, while many moths that rest on tree trunks have bark-like patterns on their wings. Even big animals like antelopes are camouflaged. Their backs are dark but underneath they

◀ Some World War I ships had
disruptive stripes to break up
their outlines against the sea.

▲ The zebra's stripes are
disruptive markings which make
it less obvious to its grassland
predators.

are usually very pale. This counteracts the shadows caused by the overhead Sun, making the animals look flat, helping them to merge into the background. Chameleons, flatfishes and prawns change colours to match different backgrounds. Stick insects take their camouflage further and actually look like twigs. This is called protective resemblance. The animals' enemies can see them, but take no notice because they are deceived.
See also NATURAL SELECTION.

Cancer

Cancer is a disease of the body CELLS in which their functioning and REPRODUCTION is uncontrolled. When a cell turns cancerous or malignant, it will not work properly, and it divides rapidly to produce more cells. A collection of cancerous cells is called a tumour. These cells are able to break away and are carried in the blood to other parts of the body, where they continue to grow.

▲ The leaf insect is the same
colour as leaves. It has leaf-like
markings on its wings, which
help camouflage it from
predators.

◀ Radiation therapy is used to
destroy cancer cells with X-rays
or particles from radioactive
elements such as cobalt-60.

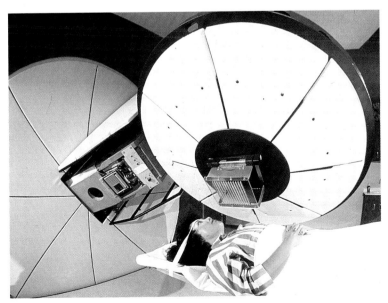

Tumour A build-up or mass of tissue where the reproductive process of the cells has gone wrong.
Benign tumour A tumour that does not spread into the surrounding healthy tissues of the body.
Malignant tumour A tumour that invades. It increases in size and eventually destroys surrounding healthy tissue.

Carcinogen A cancer-causing substance. It attacks normal cells, and may eventually cause some of them to turn cancerous.
Carcinoma Cancer that starts to grow in tissue that forms the skin and linings of inner organs.
Sarcoma Cancer that starts to grow in the tissue that forms the body's supporting structures, such as the bones and the cartilage.

Usually, cells are replaced as they become old and inefficient. The development of these new cells is controlled so that the new cells are identical to the old ones. In cancer, so many abnormal cells are produced that they interfere with normal body functions and if untreated may cause very severe illness or death.

The causes are not clear, but chemicals such as tar from cigarettes and many other substances are known to change normal cells into cancer cells. Cancer can be treated by surgery, or by very powerful DRUGS, or by radiation which damages the affected cells. Though people still die from cancer, many are surviving due to the improvement and success of modern treatments.

Canning

Canning is the most common way of preserving food. The food is sealed inside a METAL can of ALUMINIUM or thin STEEL and then heated to over 100°C. This kills any MICROORGANISMS that might spoil the food. Since the can is heated after sealing, no new organisms can affect the food before the can is opened.

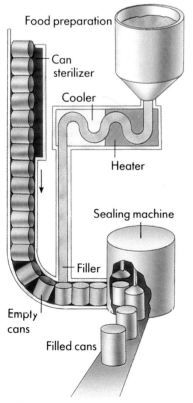

▼ *The filling and sealing of cans is generally done by machines. Modern commercial machines are able to fill up to 1200 cans in one minute.*

Food preparation

Can sterilizer

Cooler

Heater

Sealing machine

Filler

Empty cans

Filled cans

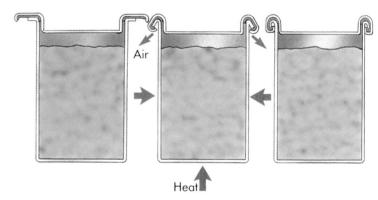

▲ *After being filled up with the prepared food, some of the air is removed from the can. It is then sealed and heated to destroy microorganisms before being rapidly cooled.*

In 1809, a Frenchman called Nicholas Appert successfully preserved food by sealing it inside a glass container. The containers were easily broken and unsuitable for packaging food. The following year Peter Durand, an Englishman, produced the first TIN cans which were used for food storage. Foods of many different kinds are canned in canning factories. The first canning factory was opened in 1819 in the United States and soldiers in the American Civil War (1861–1865) ate canned food.

Capacitor

Capacitors store electrical charge; they used to be called condensers. The simplest capacitor consists of two metal plates separated by an electrical INSULATOR. Positive charge is stored on one plate and negative charge on the other. The amount of charge the device can store for a given voltage difference is called the *capacitance*; for the capacitance to be large, the plates have to be large and close together.

Capacitors can smooth the flow of a fluctuating current and variable capacitors are used in circuits that tune

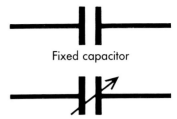

▲ *The standard symbols for fixed and variable capacitors are used in circuit diagrams. Variable capacitors have movable plates.*

◀ *Capacitors are just one of the components of electric circuits. In a capacitor, the size of the metal plates and the distance they are apart decides how much electrical charge they can store.*

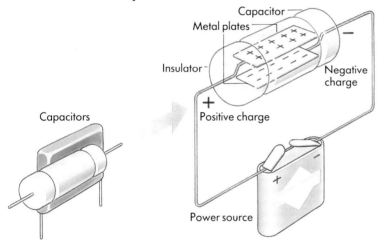

a radio or television to the required station. Capacitors can also block the flow of a direct current and allow an alternating current to pass.
See also CIRCUIT, ELECTRIC; ELECTRICITY.

Capillary action

Capillary action is the process which causes LIQUID in the soil to rise up through the roots and stems of plants and water to seep through a paper towel. If one end of a narrow tube is placed in water, the water rises up the tube; the narrower the tube the higher the water will rise. This is caused by an attraction between the MOLECULES at the surface of the liquid and the molecules of the glass of the tube. It is called SURFACE TENSION. The liquid rises until the weight of the liquid balances the surface tension.

When liquid molecules at the surface attract each other more than they do the wall of the tube, surface tension causes the liquid to be depressed. Mercury acts like this. It sinks in a narrow glass tube.

SEE FOR YOURSELF
Split the stem of a flower, such as a carnation. Place one end of the stem into a jar of coloured water and the other end into another jar. The flower 'sucks up' the water through narrow tubes in its stem. The capilliary action overcomes the pull of gravity.

$C_nH_{2n}O_n$

▲ *Many carbohydrates have this general formula. The* n *stands for a number; for example, in glucose the* n *is 6 – glucose has the formula* $C_6H_{12}O_6$.

Common Sources of Carbohydrates:
Sugars: syrup, sweets, cake, muesli, chocolate, ice cream, ketchup, fruit, cola.
Starches: potatoes, bread, cake, flour, spaghetti, rice.
Fibre: muesli, branflakes, fruit, vegetables, brown rice, nuts.

Carbohydrate

Carbohydrates are chemical COMPOUNDS containing only the elements carbon, hydrogen and oxygen. There is little carbohydrate present in the body, and we obtain this important food substance from plants. The various SUGARS are carbohydrates and are an important source of ENERGY in our food. They are easily absorbed from the digestive system where they are converted into glucose and fructose, which release energy when broken down by oxygen. Starch is also a carbohydrate, but must be broken down by digestive ENZYMES into simpler sugars before it can be absorbed. This process begins in the mouth, with the enzymes in the saliva. If you chew a piece of bread for a few minutes, you will notice that it begins to taste sweet. This happens because the starch in the flour used to make the bread is gradually being converted by enzymes into sugar. A carbohydrate called CELLULOSE, commonly known as fibre, helps to keep the bowels healthy. It consists mostly of the cell walls remaining in plant foods. These cannot be digested, and pass through the system almost unchanged.

Rice

Polished rice grains

Sugar beet

Caster sugar

Sugar cane

Sugar cubes

Potatoes

Bananas

Chips

Spaghetti

Bread

Flour

Pasta

Wheat

▲ *Carbohydrates are formed in green plants during photosynthesis and are a vital source of fuel for both plants and animals. About half the food we eat should be made up of carbohydrates.*

Carbon cycle

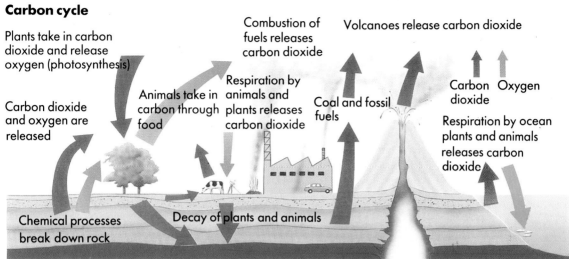

Plants take in carbon dioxide and release oxygen (photosynthesis)

Combustion of fuels releases carbon dioxide

Volcanoes release carbon dioxide

Carbon dioxide and oxygen are released

Animals take in carbon through food

Respiration by animals and plants releases carbon dioxide

Coal and fossil fuels

Carbon dioxide   Oxygen

Respiration by ocean plants and animals releases carbon dioxide

Chemical processes break down rock

Decay of plants and animals

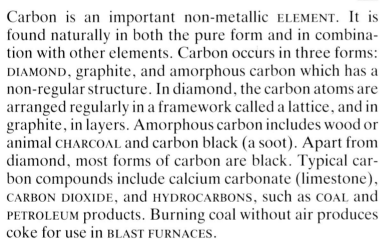

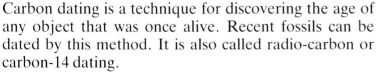

Carbon

Carbon is an important non-metallic ELEMENT. It is found naturally in both the pure form and in combination with other elements. Carbon occurs in three forms: DIAMOND, graphite, and amorphous carbon which has a non-regular structure. In diamond, the carbon atoms are arranged regularly in a framework called a lattice, and in graphite, in layers. Amorphous carbon includes wood or animal CHARCOAL and carbon black (a soot). Apart from diamond, most forms of carbon are black. Typical carbon compounds include calcium carbonate (limestone), CARBON DIOXIDE, and HYDROCARBONS, such as COAL and PETROLEUM products. Burning coal without air produces coke for use in BLAST FURNACES.

Compounds containing carbon, hydrogen and certain other elements make up the living tissues in all plants and animals and are studied in ORGANIC CHEMISTRY.

▲ The carbon cycle is a constant exchange of carbon between the atmosphere and plants and animals. Carbon dioxide is taken in by plants during photosynthesis. These plants are in turn eaten by animals. Carbon dioxide is given out during respiration.

▼ Carbon has two crystalline forms, diamond and graphite. Diamond is one of the hardest known solids and graphite is one of the softest.

Diamond

Graphite

Carbon dating

Carbon dating is a technique for discovering the age of any object that was once alive. Recent fossils can be dated by this method. It is also called radio-carbon or carbon-14 dating.

The nucleus of a carbon atom usually contains 12 particles (the MASS NUMBER), six protons and six neutrons. Sometimes carbon atoms with a mass number of 14 are formed. Carbon-14 is radioactive because it is unstable and breaks down, or decays, very slowly into other

For more than 40 years many scientists believed that the 'missing link' between modern humans and apes had been found. Parts of a skull and jawbone thought to be more than 250,000 years old were found at Piltdown in Sussex, England between 1908 and 1912. Carbon dating of the skull in 1955 showed that the Piltdown Man was a hoax.

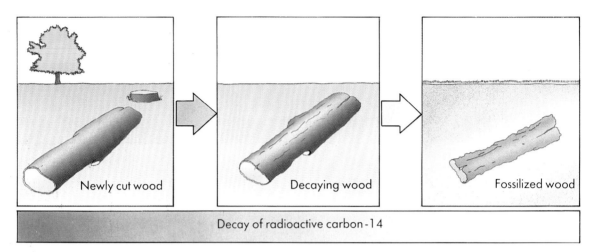

Newly cut wood

Decaying wood

Fossilized wood

Decay of radioactive carbon-14

▲ *The age of an archeological object can be estimated by measuring the amount of carbon-14 it contains. This is because carbon-14 decays constantly. After 70,000 years it will have decayed almost completely.*

▲ *Carbon dioxide is a compound of two parts of oxygen to one of carbon. The bubbles in fizzy drinks are carbon dioxide. Also, because things cannot burn in carbon dioxide, it is used in fire extinguishers.*

ELEMENTS. It has a HALF-LIFE of 5730 years. Carbon-14 in the ATMOSPHERE is taken in by plants which are eaten by animals. When plants or animals die, the carbon-14 inside them begins to decay at a constant rate. The age of any once-living object can therefore be discovered by measuring the amount of carbon-14 it still contains.

Carbon dioxide

Carbon dioxide is a colourless, odourless GAS. It makes up less than one percent of the Earth's ATMOSPHERE and is found in the atmospheres of other PLANETS, notably Mars and Venus. Carbon dioxide is formed when compounds called carbonates (containing CARBON and OXYGEN) are heated or treated with an acid and also when coal, oil, wood and other carbon compounds are burned. Animals produce carbon dioxide and release it into the air when breathing out. Plants convert carbon dioxide into oxygen by PHOTOSYNTHESIS. Carbon dioxide absorbs heat and traps it near the Earth's surface. *See also* GREENHOUSE EFFECT.

SEE FOR YOURSELF
Make a hole in a cork. Push a tube through it. Put some bicarbonate of soda and vinegar into the bottle and quickly cork it up. Collect the gas that is formed by placing an upside-down jar over the end of the tube. Move the upside-down jar over a small flame. The flame goes out because it cannot burn in carbon dioxide.

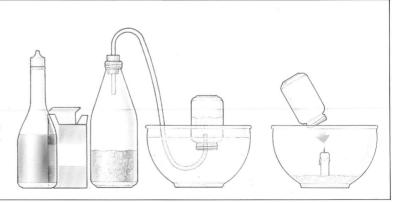

Carbon fibres

Carbon fibres are light, very strong, silk-like fibres of pure carbon made by stretching and heating textile fibres. They can stand very great strains without breaking and keep their strength even at high TEMPERATURES. Compared with the steel used in making aircraft, carbon fibres are about a quarter of the WEIGHT but twice as strong. They are used chiefly for reinforcing plastics, ceramics and metals, especially turbine blades.

▲ Individual carbon fibres are combined with plastic to give a composite material that is both strong and light.

◄ The aerospace industry is one of the largest users of materials containing carbon fibres. This Beechcraft starship aircraft is unusual because its body is made from layers of carbon fibres with other materials in between.

Carbon monoxide

Carbon monoxide is a colourless, tasteless, odourless and extremely poisonous GAS. It is given off when CARBON is burned in a restricted air supply. When oxygen is plentiful, the much less dangerous CARBON DIOXIDE is formed. People who accidentally breathe in carbon monoxide can lose consciousness. Traffic fumes and cigarette smoke contain carbon monoxide, and in busy streets there may be a dangerous build-up of carbon monoxide in the atmosphere. Carbon monoxide is used in certain industrial processes, such as the separation of iron and other metals from ORES.

CO

▲ Carbon monoxide is a compound of carbon and oxygen. It has half as much oxygen as carbon dioxide. It is formed when substances containing carbon are burned in a very small air supply.

Carver, George Washington See Agriculture

▶ *Portable cassette recorders contain all the components needed to enable cassettes to be played, including the cassette drive, speakers and an amplifier.*

▼ *Modern micro-electronics has made it possible to build radio-cassette players that are small enough to be carried in a pocket. The cassette players do not have speakers so you need to use headphones to listen to the sound.*

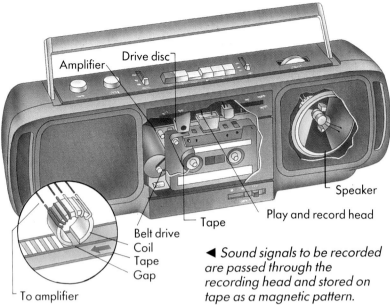

Amplifier — Drive disc

Speaker

Play and record head

Tape

Belt drive
Coil
Tape
Gap

To amplifier

◀ *Sound signals to be recorded are passed through the recording head and stored on tape as a magnetic pattern.*

Cassette recorder

A cassette recorder is a machine used to record SOUND and play it back through a LOUDSPEAKER or headphones. The sounds are recorded on a strip of flexible plastic tape wound onto tiny reels housed in a cassette. Most cassette tapes are coated with iron oxide. The particles of iron oxide normally lie randomly, pointing in different directions. To record sound, it is first changed into an electric current by a MICROPHONE. The current changes the strength of the magnetic field produced by a recording and playback head. As the tape travels past the head, the changing magnetic field makes the magnetic particles in the tape line up together. To listen to the recording, the tape is rewound. As it passes the head again, the magnetic particles in the tape produce currents in the head which are amplified into the original sound.

Cast iron

The Chinese produced cast iron as early as the 6th century BC, but it did not reach Europe until the 12th century AD. In the 19th century it formed the basis for the very first skyscrapers. The most famous cast iron building was the Crystal Palace. It was designed by Joseph Paxton for the Great Exhibition of 1851 in London.

Cast iron is the general name given to various ALLOYS of IRON. It is a poor-quality yet strong type of iron. Each type of cast iron has its own composition and qualities and is made up of varying amounts of iron, carbon, silicon and smaller amounts of manganese, phosphorus and sulphur. It contains so much carbon that it is too brittle to be worked into shape by FORGING. It is only possible to shape cast iron in its liquid state when it can be formed into objects using moulds, a process called CASTING. Cast iron is used for decorative ironwork and objects such as car engines, which need to be strong.

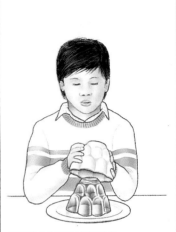

◄ *Iron must be heated in a furnace to very high temperatures so that it becomes liquid. It can then be poured into moulds for casting.*

SEE FOR YOURSELF
Pour some jelly mixture into a mould. When the jelly has set, place the bottom of the mould in a bowl of hot water for a few seconds. Turn the jelly mould over onto a plate. Tap it and lift the mould off the jelly, which appears cast in the shape of the mould.

Casting

Casting is the process used to shape objects by pouring a liquid into a mould and letting it harden. It is used to produce objects in plastic, iron, steel, aluminium and ceramics.

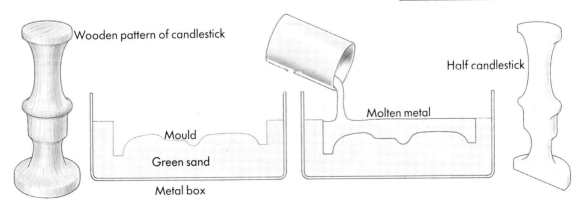

Wooden pattern of candlestick

Half candlestick

Molten metal

Mould

Green sand

Metal box

The first stage is to make a model of the object to be cast. This may be of wood or some other material. Some articles may need to be cast in more than one piece. The model is then placed in a special moulding box called a flask. Moulds for objects with spaces in the middle have a small hole through which the material can be poured.

▲ *The casting process is made up of three stages. A model, or pattern, of the finished object is made. A mould is made by packing sand round the pattern and then removing the pattern to leave a hollow. Finally the molten metal is poured in.*

Metal objects are usually cast in sand moulds. Damp sand is packed tightly round the model to fill the space between it and the walls of the flask. The model is then removed and the molten metal is poured into the mould. Once the metal has cooled and hardened, the mould is broken open to reveal the cast object.

Catalysts in plants and animals are called enzymes. They are protein molecules which speed up the chemical reactions without which life would be impossible. Enzymes break down substances into simpler substances. A single enzyme molecule can perform its entire function a million times a minute. The human body has over 1000 kinds of enzyme. Enzymes in the digestive system, for example, break down food for use in the body.

Catalyst

A catalyst is a substance that speeds up a reaction between two other substances without itself being changed or used up by the reaction. Catalysts are very important in the industrial production of certain chemical substances. The process by which they work is known as catalysis. In most CHEMICAL REACTIONS there are several possible sequences of steps through which the reactions can proceed. Catalysts take part in some or all of these steps. They help reactions to take place more quickly and more efficiently than they otherwise would, for example, heated IRON is used as a catalyst that speeds up the combination of hydrogen and nitrogen in the industrial manufacture of AMMONIA. Chemicals called ENZYMES are catalysts that speed up and encourage complicated chemical reactions in all animals and plants.

SEE FOR YOURSELF
Put a sugar cube into a glass of lemonade or other fizzy drink. This causes the fizzy drink to fizz up violently. This is an example of a physical catalyst. The sugar cube provides lots of sites for bubble formation on the sharp sugar crystals, which dramatically increases the number of bubbles of carbon dioxide inside the glass.

Catalytic converter

A catalytic converter is designed to reduce the amount of harmful gases pumped into the ATMOSPHERE by vehicle engines. The converter is a METAL case containing a metal or CERAMIC honeycomb coated with a precious metal such as platinum, palladium or rhodium which is the CATALYST. A honeycomb is used because it enables a

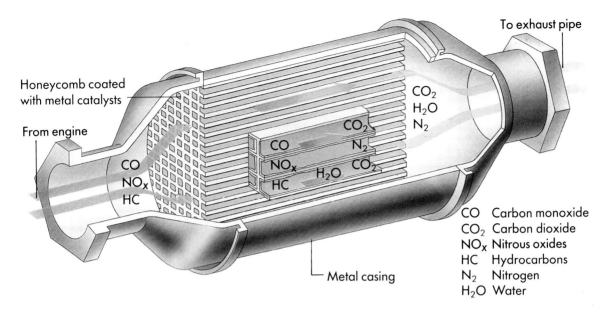

To exhaust pipe

Honeycomb coated with metal catalysts

From engine

CO
NOx
HC

CO
CO
NOx
HC

CO₂
N₂
H₂O
CO₂

CO₂
H₂O
N₂

Metal casing

CO   Carbon monoxide
CO₂ Carbon dioxide
NOₓ Nitrous oxides
HC   Hydrocarbons
N₂   Nitrogen
H₂O Water

very high surface area to be packed into a small volume. The converter is fitted to the vehicle's exhaust pipe. As the engine's exhaust gases flow through the honeycomb, the catalyst produces CHEMICAL REACTIONS among the gases that change the harmful ingredients (carbon monoxide, oxides of nitrogen, and hydrocarbons) into water vapour and carbon dioxide. A converter works most efficiently when the mixture of fuel and air supplied to the engine is carefully monitored and adjusted by a computerized engine management system.

▲ *All new cars will eventually be required by law to have pollution-reducing catalytic converters fitted to their exhausts.*

Cathode *See* Electrolysis

Cathode ray tube

A cathode ray tube is a tube, usually made of glass, from which most of the air has been removed and inside which a beam of ELECTRONS is produced. The beam comes from an electron gun made of a piece of heated METAL kept at a negative voltage. This repels the electrons which are emitted from the surface and a series of positive grids accelerates them to a high speed. The piece of hot metal is known as the cathode after the negative electrode in ELECTROLYSIS.

Very narrow beams of electrons can now be produced. If the far end of the tube is covered with luminescent paint, the beam then produces a small spot of light. Electric defining plates or magnetic deflecting rings are used to bend the beam, so the spot traces an image. The paint continues to glow for a short time after

William Crookes (1832–1919) Crookes was a British physicist and chemist. In 1861, he discovered the element thallium. His studies on electrical discharges in vacuum tubes resulted in the Crookes tube, an early cathode ray tube, in 1880. He found that 'cathode rays' cast shadows and travelled in straight lines, which could be deflected by a magnet. He believed that cathode rays were made up of negatively-charged particles (electrons).

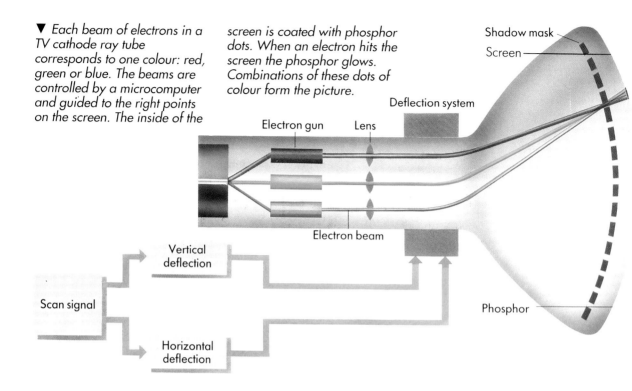

▼ Each beam of electrons in a TV cathode ray tube corresponds to one colour: red, green or blue. The beams are controlled by a microcomputer and guided to the right points on the screen. The inside of the screen is coated with phosphor dots. When an electron hits the screen the phosphor glows. Combinations of these dots of colour form the picture.

Shadow mask
Screen
Deflection system
Electron gun
Lens
Electron beam
Vertical deflection
Scan signal
Horizontal deflection
Phosphor

the spot has moved on, so our eyes do not see the movement. This is how pictures are produced by a TELEVISION or an OSCILLOSCOPE. Colour pictures can be made by using luminescent paints which glow different colours. The first cathode ray tube was made by Sir William Crookes in 1880.

See also COLOUR; LUMINESCENCE.

NaOH

▲ The chemical formula for sodium hydroxide or caustic soda. Sodium hydroxide is often produced by the electrolysis of sodium chloride or salt.

Caustic soda

Caustic soda is sodium hydroxide, a chemical compound formed from SODIUM, HYDROGEN and OXYGEN. Caustic soda is a very dangerous compound. 'Caustic' means 'burning' and caustic substances will burn or eat away other substances, especially organic materials, including human body tissues. Caustic soda should never be allowed to come into contact with the skin, mouth or any other part of the body. In laboratories, where necessary, it should be handled with great care. Caustic soda is a strong alkali. It is used to make soap and is an efficient drain cleaner because it attacks grease and other waste matter blocking pipes.

CD-ROM See Multimedia

CELL 🏃

A cell is the smallest living unit which is able to carry out all the basic functions of life: growth, metabolism and reproduction. Some simple organisms consist of a single cell, while most plants and animals are constructed from huge numbers of cells, adapted to perform particular functions. But even in these multicellular organisms, the individual cells are capable of growing, feeding and reproducing.

A typical cell consists of *cytoplasm*, a watery, jelly-like material, surrounded by a thin membrane which helps to give the cell its shape but allows various substances to pass through. Oxygen and food substances enter the cell in this way, and waste products are removed. Plant cells also have a cell wall, made of cellulose, which can sometimes be very thick and so gives the plant its shape. Vertebrate animals are supported by a hard skeleton produced by bone cells.

The nucleus is a dense body within the cytoplasm containing the chromosomes and genes which govern the cell and the way it works. It can be seen under a microscope.

Most of the chemical reactions which power and maintain the body take place in the cell. Small structures called organelles are present in the cytoplasm, and these tiny chemical factories produce hormones, enzymes and other substances which are released for use in the cell and elsewhere in the body.

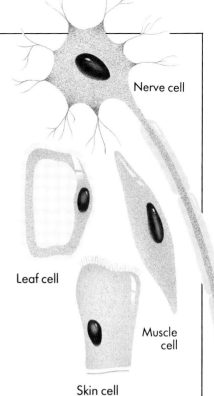

Nerve cell

Leaf cell

Muscle cell

Skin cell

▲ A human consists of many millions of cells. Nerves and muscles, for example, are made up of specialized cells.

◀ Animal cells contain a number of different organelles that carry out the chemical processes required for life. Lysosomes contain enzymes that can help white blood cells break down harmful bacteria.

▼ Plant cells have a cell wall made of cellulose which animal cells do not. Vacuoles are fluid-filled cavities common in plant cells.

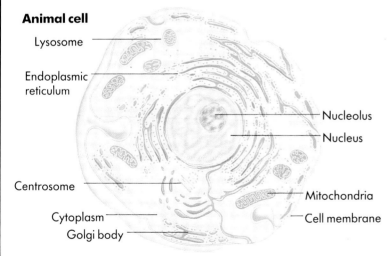

Animal cell

- Lysosome
- Endoplasmic reticulum
- Nucleolus
- Nucleus
- Centrosome
- Mitochondria
- Cytoplasm
- Cell membrane
- Golgi body

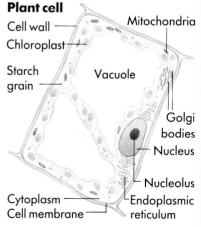

Plant cell

- Cell wall
- Chloroplast
- Starch grain
- Vacuole
- Mitochondria
- Golgi bodies
- Nucleus
- Nucleolus
- Cytoplasm
- Cell membrane
- Endoplasmic reticulum

Centrosome This contains the centrioles that are important in cell division.
Endoplasmic reticulum These contain the units where protein is made.
Golgi bodies Involved in the secretion of cell products and may also help in protein manufacture.
Mitochondria Tiny rod-shaped structures with a tightly-folded inner membrane where glucose is broken down to keep the cell supplied with energy.

See also BIOLOGY; BONE; CELL DIVISION; CELLULOSE; CHROMOSOMES AND GENES; CYTOLOGY; GENETICS; MICROSCOPE; NUCLEUS, CELL; OXYGEN; REPRODUCTION.

Cell division

▼ *Meiosis is the process by which male and female sex cells are formed. It produces cells with only half the number of chromosomes. This means that when a male and female sex cell combine during sexual reproduction, the new cell that is formed will have the normal number of chromosomes. Both animal and plant cells divide in the same way.*
1 Bodies in the cell called centrioles move to opposite sides of the nucleus. The chromosomes appear as long threads. 2 A structure called a spindle starts to form from the centrioles. 3 The chromosomes become shorter and fatter and pair up. 4 Each chromosome copies itself and divides into two strands called chromatids joined at the centre. 5 The

Cells divide when they have grown larger than is necessary for them to carry out their normal function, or when they reach the end of their lifespan. Cell division is seen most easily in simple microscopic animals, for example the amoeba, which is a single cell. When ready to divide, it simply splits in half, dividing the contents of the CELL equally. Most simple plants and animals divide like this. In more complex organisms, a process called *mitosis* is used, which makes sure that the information in the genes is shared equally between the new 'daughter' cells. All this material is in the cell nucleus, stored on thread-like CHROMOSOMES. The chromosomes are in pairs, and during cell division these pairs are separated and move to opposite sides of the cell. The cell now divides into two, and the chromosomes are doubled again. A similar process called *meiosis* takes place when the body produces sperm and eggs, except that in this case, the chromosomes are not doubled until after FERTILIZATION. All the cells in the body are able to divide except for nerve cells, which last throughout life.

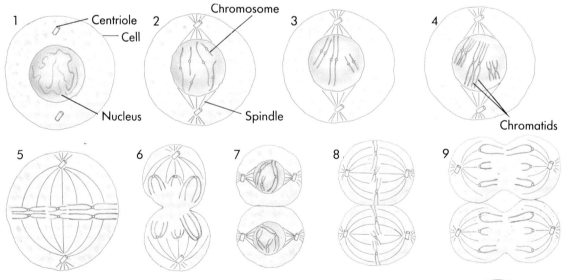

chromosomes become arranged across the middle of the cell. *6 The pairs of chromosomes split apart and go to opposite sides of the cell, and the cell divides once. 7 A resting period follows before the cycle is repeated, 8 and 9. This time the pairs of chromatids split* apart and move to opposite sides of the cell, and the cells divide again *10. Each one of the four new cells has half the number of chromosomes that were in the original cell. At fertilization, two cells fuse together so the embryo has a full set of chromosomes.*

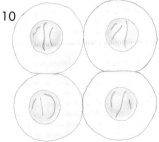

Cellular radio and telephones

Cellular RADIO and TELEPHONES are used for COMMUNI-CATION. Telephones are connected by cable, and cordless telephones allow the user to move only a few metres

▼ The cellular telephone network area is divided up into cells. When a cell phone user makes a call, a radio signal is sent to the nearest base station. This is sent to the nearest mobile telephone exchange. The call is then directed to either another telephone network or to another subscriber.

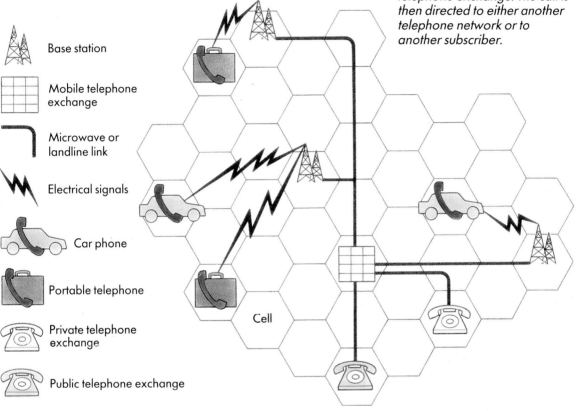

Base station

Mobile telephone exchange

Microwave or landline link

Electrical signals

Car phone

Portable telephone

Private telephone exchange

Public telephone exchange

Cell

from the base station. A cellular phone can be used almost anywhere. The country is covered by a grid of radio cells, areas where a particular radio channel or transmitting FREQUENCY is used. A relay station in each cell handles transmissions from all the telephones in that cell. If the telephone user moves into another cell, a new relay station takes over. Because the cells are small, the same small number of radio channels can be used again and again. The second generation cellular telephone network uses only 40 channels. The two first generation cellular phone systems, in Britain called Cellnet and Vodafone, transmit speech as ANALOGUE radio signals. The second generation systems are all DIGITAL and suffer less from interference.

▼ With a compact cellular telephone you can make and receive calls anywhere within the cellular network.

Celluloid *See* Plastics

▶ *This greatly magnified criss-cross pattern of fibres is of cellulose microfibrils. They form a large part of the surface of a leaf.*

▼ *The cell wall of a plant cell is made up mainly of cellulose, which gives a plant its firm structure.*

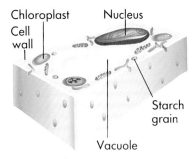

Chloroplast   Nucleus
Cell
wall

Starch
grain

Vacuole

In the 1850s chemists first dissolved wood pulp and cotton fibres to obtain the cellulose in them. Fibres of cellulose were first made in 1855 by Georges Audemars of Switzerland. Unfortunately, the chemical process he used turned the cellulose into nitrocellulose, a powerful explosive. Fabrics made from it burst into flames very easily.

▲ *Anders Celsius (1701–1744), a Swedish astronomer, suggested that temperature should be measured on what we now call the Celsius scale.*

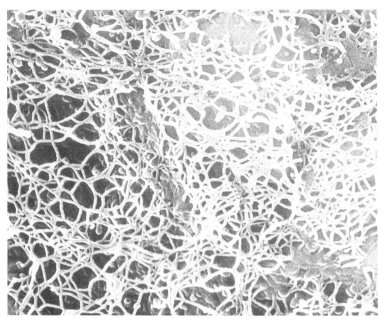

Cellulose

Cellulose is a CARBOHYDRATE and is an important part of plant CELLS, where it makes up most of the material in the cell wall. It is a very tough substance, made up from long molecules which are laid down in a crisscross pattern, giving strength and rigidity to the cell. Cotton and linen fabrics consist almost entirely of cellulose which is naturally formed in long fibres. *Viscose* is a form of processed cellulose commonly used to make fabrics and clothes. Humans are unable to digest cellulose, which makes up most of the fibre in our diet. However, animals such as sheep, cattle and rabbits have specially adapted digestive systems. This allows them to use the cellulose which they obtain from the grass they eat. Bacteria in their digestive systems break down the cellulose into simpler SUGARS, which are easily absorbed.

Celsius

The Celsius scale is one of the systems for measuring TEMPERATURE. It is named after Anders Celsius and is sometimes called the Centigrade scale. On this scale the normal FREEZING POINT of water is at 0 degrees and the normal BOILING POINT at 100 degrees. It is the standard scale for measuring temperature in countries which use the METRIC SYSTEM. To convert a temperature in degrees Celsius to a temperature in FAHRENHEIT, multiply by nine and divide by five, then add 32 (to reverse the conversion, subtract 32, multiply by five and divide by nine).

The choice of zero degrees on the Celsius scale is only made out of convenience, because WATER is such a common substance on the Earth. The fundamental scale of temperature is the KELVIN scale, in which water freezes at 273.16 K. The zero temperature on the Kelvin scale is called absolute zero (−273.16°C).

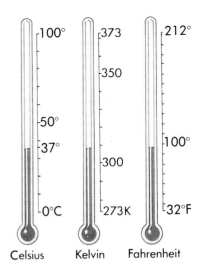

Celsius   Kelvin   Fahrenheit

▲ Normal body temperature in humans is 37°C on the Celsius scale, 310 K using the Kelvin scale and 98.6°F on the Fahrenheit scale.

Cement

Cement is a material used to stick objects together. The paste used to stick wallpaper to walls and the glue used to build plastic kits are both types of cement. In the CONSTRUCTION industry, cement is made from limestone and clay. These are mixed together and roasted. The dry 'clinker' produced is mixed with a material called gypsum (calcium sulphate) and ground into a fine powder. This cement is mixed with sand and water to make mortar for sticking bricks together. It is also mixed with sand, gravel and water to make concrete. Cement and water react together chemically, making the mortar or concrete harden. After this, water does not affect it.

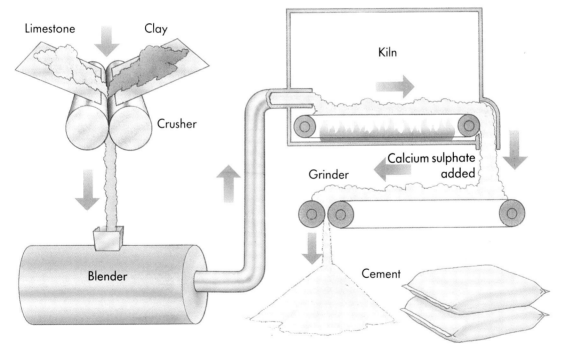

▲ To make cement, water is added to a mixture of chalk from limestone rock and clay. This mixture is heated to 1400°C in a rotating kiln, cooled, mixed with calcium sulphate and ground to a fine powder.

Centigrade *See* Celsius

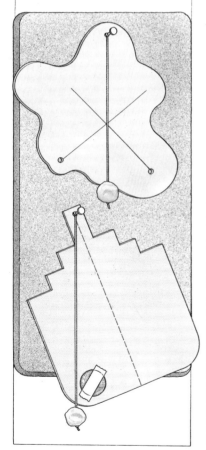

▶ *Part of the excitement of this fairground ride comes from being pulled up and away from the centre of rotation. This is because of the centrifugal force.*

106

Centre of gravity

The force of GRAVITY acts on all parts of an object, but it is often helpful to think of it as a FORCE applied at a single point. This point is called the centre of gravity; you can think of it as the average position of all the particles that make up the body. It is also known as the centre of mass. If an object is balanced or hung so it does not fall over, the BALANCING POINT must be exactly below the centre of gravity so that the gravitational force and the supporting force exactly cancel each other out and do not cause the body to turn and fall over. If the centre of gravity is not over the balancing point of an object, the object is not stable and will turn and fall over.

Centrifugal force

Centrifugal force occurs when an object is spinning fast. It is the FORCE that appears to push everything to the out-side of the spinning circle, but in fact it is a reaction to the *centripetal force* which is acting towards the centre of the circle. You can see the centrifugal effect when you whirl an object on a string around your head. You are pulling the object towards you with the string. The force you are creating pulling inwards is the centripetal force. The object is reacting to the centripetal force and seems to be pulling outwards away from you. If the centripetal force stops (for example, if you let go of the string) the centri-fugal force also stops and the object will fly off in a

straight line, following the direction it was moving at the time you let go of the string.

It is because of the centrifugal force that a bucket of water can be whirled round in a circle without spilling. You can feel the centrifugal force yourself in a car going round a corner or in fairground rides.

There is another force, called the Coriolis force; you can feel it trying to pull you to one side if you walk towards the centre of a roundabout while it is turning. This force is an important influence on the airflow in the ATMOSPHERE.

Centrifuge

A centrifuge is a machine used to spin substances at a high speed. Scientists often use centrifuges to separate particles from a liquid or to divide a mixture of liquids into its different ingredients. The mixture is placed in a tube which pivots so that when the machine starts to move, the tube can swing out horizontally. The CENTRIFUGAL FORCE tries to push the mixture away from the centre of the centrifuge. The heavier particles or liquid move further outwards (towards the bottom of the mixture). When the centrifuge is stopped, the materials stay in this unmixed state. Blood and other biological samples are often separated by centrifuge. The fastest centrifuges, called ultracentrifuges, spin at up to 200,000 revolutions per minute. Large centrifuges are used to test military pilots and ASTRONAUTS who have to be able to withstand high accelerations.

▼ Laboratory centrifuges are used to separate substances. A type of centrifuge is used to train astronauts. They are whirled round so they experience the same forces as when a rocket blasts off.

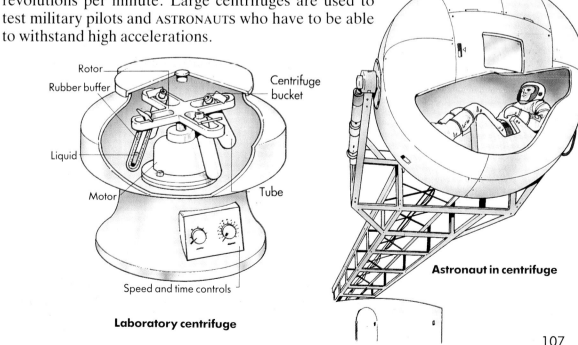

Rotor, Rubber buffer, Centrifuge bucket, Liquid, Motor, Tube, Speed and time controls

Laboratory centrifuge

Astronaut in centrifuge

▲ *This softball bat has a very strong ceramic coating. The ceramic will not split, chip or wear away so the bat will last longer than a wooden one.*

▶ *Ceramic engine casings are being developed. They are very strong and can withstand high temperatures. They are lighter than the cast iron ones which are commonly used.*

Nutrients in Cereals:
Carbohydrates, for energy; **Protein**, for growth and maintenance of bones, skin and muscles; **Calcium**, for growth and maintenance of bones and teeth; **Iron**, for the blood; **Vitamin A**, for development of skin and bones; **Vitamin C**, for the development of tissue, ligaments and tendons; **Vitamin B$_1$**, used to break down starches and sugars in the body; **Vitamin B$_2$** and **Niacin**, used by the body to break down food into useful substances.

Ceramics

Ceramics are hard, brittle materials made from clay. When the clay has been moulded or shaped, it is heated in a kiln until it hardens. Ceramics are resistant to the action of water and most chemicals. They also have a high resistance to electric currents and so they can be used in electrical systems as INSULATORS. There are several different types of ceramic materials. Enamels and POTTERY AND PORCELAIN are examples. Heavy clay ceramics include bricks, underground drain pipes and roofing tiles used in construction. Some ceramics with a particularly high MELTING POINT are used to make the bricks that line furnaces and also parts of spacecraft that have to withstand high temperatures.

Ceramics have been replaced in many cases by PLASTICS that are more resistant to damage and can be moulded into more complicated shapes. However, research has resulted in new ceramics and manufacturers of car and aircraft engines are experimenting with ceramic parts that wear out more slowly than metal and can stand very high temperatures.

Cereals

Cereals are large grasses which are cultivated for their nutritious SEEDS (grain). They provide the staple food for people in nearly every part of the world. The grain is rich in energy-giving STARCH and also contains valuable amounts of PROTEIN, VITAMINS, and dietary fibre (as you

World map of cereal production

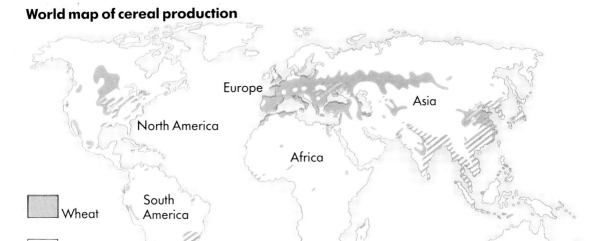

Europe

Asia

North America

Africa

Wheat

South
America

Maize

Rice

Australasia

will see from your breakfast cereal packet). Wheat, rice and maize are the most important cereals. Between them they cover over half of the world's cultivated land and yield about 1,000,000,000 tonnes of grain every year. Not all this is for human food; much of it goes to feed cattle and other livestock. Other important cereals include barley, oats, rye, sorghum and millet.

Cereals have been cultivated for about 10,000 years and now look very different from the wild grasses from which they are descended. Early farmers gradually increased the size and quality of their crops simply by sowing seed from the biggest and best plants every year, and plant-breeders have made further huge improvements during the 20th century using modern HORTICULTURE and BREEDING techniques.

See also AGRICULTURE; GENETICS; HEREDITY.

CERN

CERN (*Conseil Européen pour la Recherche Nucléaire*) is one of Europe's most important PHYSICS research laboratories. Founded in 1954, it is located near Geneva on the border between France and Switzerland.

CERN uses massive machines called PARTICLE ACCELERATORS to study the structure of MATTER. The aluminium pipe of CERN's latest accelerator, the Large Electron-Positron collider (LEP), is 27 km long and

▲ *Wheat is the most important cereal grain in the world followed by maize. Rice is the staple diet of over half the world's population.*

▼ *Barley, oats and maize are the main food crops where wheat and rice crops are poor.*

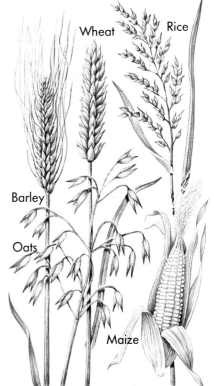

Wheat

Rice

Barley

Oats

Maize

▶ *The large circle marks the underground path of the Large Electron-Positron collider (LEP) at CERN in Switzerland.*

▼ *Chalk started to be formed millions of years ago. As sea animals and plants died, they sank to the bottom of the sea and formed a layer of calcium deposits. In places where the sea receded these deposits formed the land. Millions of years of erosion and land movement mean that some of this chalk is now exposed.*

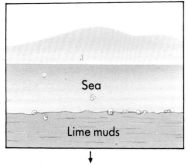

Sea

Lime muds

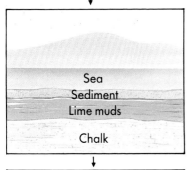

Sea
Sediment
Lime muds

Chalk

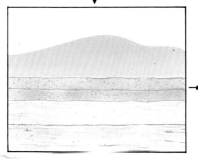

buried in a tunnel 50–150 m underground. Accelerating particles in the LEP to near-light speed requires enormous electric power. At its peak, the LEP uses enough electricity to power a city of 200,000 people. The results of its experiments are analyzed by a powerful computer. Similar experiments are being carried out at the Stanford Linear Collider (SLC) in Stanford, California.

Chain reaction *See* Nuclear energy

Chalk

Chalk is a soft, powdery white rock, consisting of CALCIUM carbonate. Like limestone rocks, it is mostly formed from the fragments of countless millions of tiny sea creatures that were deposited on the ocean bed

Chalk exposed

Erosion

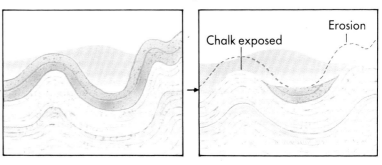

during the Cretaceous period (about 135–90 million years ago). A chalky soil indicates that the land was once almost certainly under the sea, for example, the downland and cliffs of much of southern England, Normandy in France, Texas and Kansas in the United States. Chalk is best known as a writing material (though writing chalk is usually calcium sulphate). It has many other uses, notably in the manufacture of CEMENT and FERTILIZERS.

CaCO₃

▲ *Calcium carbonate is the main compound in chalk. It is a white, crystalline mineral.*

Charcoal

Charcoal is a form of CARBON. It is a black, brittle substance and is found in two forms: wood charcoal and animal charcoal. These are made by burning wood or bone in an oven that contains little or no air. In this process, hydrogen and oxygen are driven off leaving the charcoal, together with some impurities. Wood charcoal in some cases burns well and is used as a fuel. Activated charcoal is a purified form of charcoal that is used for removing unwanted colours, flavours and smells from things. It absorbs them because it has large spaces between its atoms.

During the Roman period, charcoal and wood were the only fuels available for use in the iron, tin and copper-making industries. The wood used for producing charcoal at this time included maple, birch, plum, ash and oak.

Analysis of prehistoric pigments shows that Stone Age people used charcoal as a cosmetic.

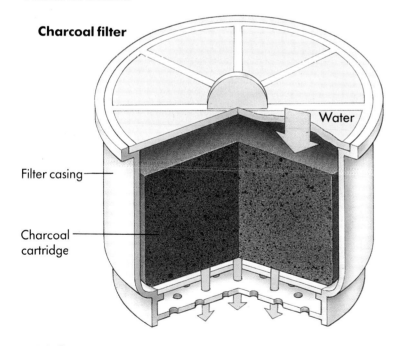

Charcoal filter

Filter casing

Charcoal cartridge

Water

◀ *Charcoal is an effective filter. It is used in water purification systems. The water is passed through a container full of charcoal which absorbs, like a sponge, the impurities and chemicals in the water.*

▼ *Many countries have dramatic chalk landforms. These cliffs are in southern Britain — the White Cliffs of Dover.*

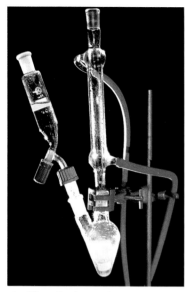

▲ *Chemical reactions are carried out and measured using a variety of complicated-looking apparatus.*

▼ *Bread rising and the digestion of food are chemical reactions just like experimental reactions in a laboratory. The reaction below produces a solid compound. The blue solids show that there is copper in the solution of copper sulphate. If more ammonia is added a further reaction takes place to give a slightly different compound with a darker colour.*

Charles, Jacques *See* Gas

Chemical reactions

A chemical reaction is a process in which one set of chemical substances, known as the reactants, are changed into another substance or set of substances, called the products. In a chemical reaction, BONDS between atoms are broken and re-formed. The products of a reaction usually have different chemical properties (appearance and behaviour) from those of the original reactants. For example, when the gases hydrogen and oxygen are ignited together with a flame, they explode and form the liquid water. Reactions such as that one between hydrogen and oxygen can be very fast. Others, such as the rusting of iron, are very slow. Many reactions take place over a measurable period of time. Chemists use chemical equations and CHEMICAL SYMBOLS to show what happens in a reaction. The formation of water from hydrogen and oxygen looks like this:

$$2H_2(g) + O_2(g) \rightarrow 2H_2O(l)$$

This shows that the gases (g) hydrogen and oxygen produce the liquid (l) water. Some reactions are reversible, which means that the reactants produce products that then recombine to produce the original reactants.

Heat will speed up a slow reaction; so will the use of a CATALYST. Light can also cause a chemical reaction, for example, light causes silver salts on photographic film to change when a photograph is being taken.

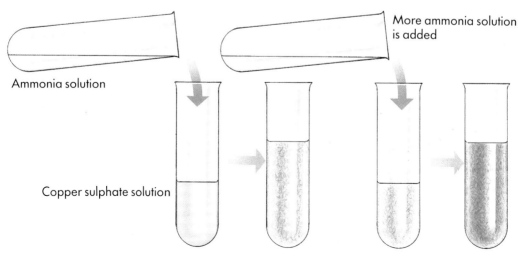

More ammonia solution is added

Ammonia solution

Copper sulphate solution

Pale blue solid forms

Dark blue solution forms

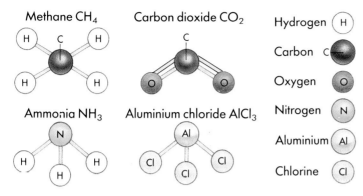

Methane CH$_4$ Carbon dioxide CO$_2$ Hydrogen H

Carbon C

Oxygen O

Ammonia NH$_3$ Aluminium chloride AlCl$_3$ Nitrogen N

Aluminium Al

Chlorine Cl

◄ *These are just some of the symbols used to stand for chemical elements. These symbols are used in chemical formulae to show combinations of elements.*

Chemical symbols

A chemical symbol is a single alphabetic letter or a pair of letters that stands for a chemical ELEMENT. Symbols are used in chemical equations and formulae and in a chart showing the PERIODIC TABLE. All the elements up to lawrencium (which has an ATOMIC NUMBER of 103) have internationally agreed symbols to go with their names. The symbol is either a capital letter (e.g. C for carbon, H for hydrogen or S for sulphur) or a capital letter followed by a small letter (e.g. Al for aluminium, Ba for barium or Ca for calcium). Usually the small letter in a two letter symbol is the second letter of the element's name, as in the above examples, but often different letters are chosen to avoid confusion. Thus calcium has the symbol Ca, but cadmium has Cd and the radioactive element californium has Cf. Some elements have symbols formed from their Latin names (e.g. iron has the symbol Fe, from ferrum; lead has Pb, from plumbum). The names of certain elements have been changed, but the symbols are made up from the older names. Thus sodium has the symbol Na, from natrium, the old name for sodium. The element tungsten used to be called wolfram and still has the symbol W. The Scottish chemist Thomas Thomson was the first to use letters for chemical symbols in an article written in 1801.
See also entries for most of the elements mentioned.

Sand and salt are both chemical compounds which chemists call silica (silicon oxide) and sodium chloride. They have the chemical formulae SiO$_2$ and NaCl. From the chemical symbols we can see that a molecule of silica is made up of a silicon atom combined with two oxygen atoms and that each salt molecule contains a sodium atom combined with a chlorine atom.

The more recently discovered elements have been named after important scientists or places where research has been carried out.
Am = Americium
Es = Einsteinium
Fr = Francium
Lr = Lawrencium
Md = Mendelevium
No = Nobelium

Chemistry

Chemistry is the scientific study of ELEMENTS and the COMPOUNDS that they make with other elements. Chemists work to describe the properties of the various substances: what they are like, how they behave, how they are affected by HEAT and PRESSURE, how they react with other substances. *See* pages 114 and 115.

About four million different chemicals have been identified. This is being added to at a rate of over 5000 every week.

CHEMISTRY

Ever since our earliest ancestors began using fire one-and-a-half million years ago, we have been able to produce and control chemical reactions to help us to observe, investigate and change the properties of substances. The ancient Greek philosopher Democritus thought that substances consisted of atoms, but Aristotle considered that all substances were different combinations of four elements (earth, air, water and fire) and that one substance could be changed into another by adjusting the balance of these elements. The medieval alchemists also believed this but in the 16th and 17th centuries, alchemy gave way to modern chemistry. Chemists realized that substances that could not be changed or broken down into other substances were the real elements. A modern atomic theory was developed and various laws were discovered about the way substances behave and how they combine. Today, chemical substances of all kinds are mined or manufactured, used for research, and for the production of detergents, dyes, cosmetics, drugs, food additives, glass, paints, paper and plastics.

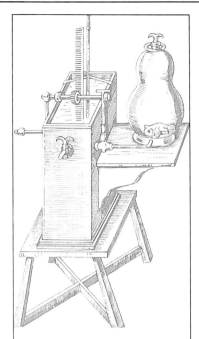

Robert Boyle (1627–1691)
Boyle was an Irish scientist. He founded the study of chemistry as a separate science and aimed to 'improve natural knowledge by experiment'. He is known for his experiments on gases and was the first chemist to isolate and collect a gas. He formulated Boyle's Law: a volume of gas at a constant temperature varies inversely with the pressure applied to the gas. He showed that air is absorbed in the process of combustion and that only one part of air, oxygen, is necessary for breathing.

SEE FOR YOURSELF
Remember to take care when handling any chemical and that any compound, even salt, can be harmful in a large enough quantity. This is a simple experiment you can do yourself. Make a hole in a cork and push a tube through it. Place some bicarbonate of soda (sodium hydrogencarbonate $NaHCO_3$) and some vinegar (weak acid) into a bottle and quickly cork it up. Place the tube in a bowl of water and watch the reaction produce bubbles of carbon dioxide gas.

Many of the discoveries made by chemists have resulted in the production of new substances from carbon compounds that have been of huge value to humans. These have included antibiotics, vitamins, hormones and drugs for medicine; pesticides for agriculture; dyes, and a wide range of artificial materials such as plastics and rubbers for the manufacturing industries.

Antoine Lavoisier (1743–1794)
Lavoisier was a French chemist. He correctly explained the role of oxygen in combustion. By carefully weighing and analysing materials after burning, he showed that burned materials are heavier than unburned materials. This was because of the addition of a gas, discovered by Scheele and Priestley. Lavoisier named it oxygen.

▲ Experiments are an interesting and fun part of a chemistry lesson. An electric current will flow through some solutions and when it does the circuit is completed and the bulb will light. Electrical conduction in solutions is called electrolysis.

▼ A polymer is a giant molecule formed from many small units. A nylon molecule is an example of a polymer. It is formed from carbon, nitrogen, hydrogen and oxygen. Models are made of molecules to show how the different atoms are joined together.

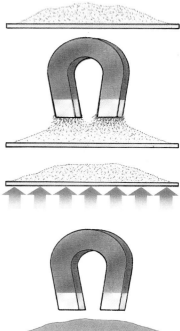

▲ When iron is mixed with sulphur, it can be removed again using a magnet. If, however, the mixture of iron and sulphur is heated, a chemical reaction takes place forming iron sulphide which is not attracted to the magnet.

Nylon molecule

Carbon   Nitrogen

Hydrogen

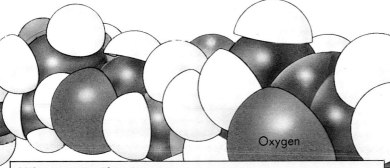

Oxygen

Milestones in Chemistry
c.3500 BC People smelting metal and making glass.
c.400 BC Democritus proposes an atomic theory.
1661 Boyle introduces modern idea of elements.
1766 Cavendish discovers hydrogen.
1770s Scheele and Priestley discover oxygen.
1828 Wöhler makes first synthetic organic substance from inorganic compounds.
1869 Mendeleyev and Lothar Meyer discover periodic law.
1913 Bohr proposes a model of the atom.
1916 Lewis describes electronic bonding between atoms.
1953 DNA and RNA found to affect heredity.
1980s Chemists work to develop a chemical cell that produces hydrogen fuel by the chemical breakdown of water.

See also ATOM; CHEMICAL REACTION; INORGANIC CHEMISTRY; MOLECULE; ORGANIC CHEMISTRY; PERIODIC TABLE.

▲ *During World War I, chlorine gas was the first method of chemical warfare to be used. The first attack caught many troops unprepared. Gas masks were eventually issued to troops to reduce the number of people suffering from severe respiratory problems.*

▶ *Chlorine gas is manufactured by passing an electric current through a solution of sodium chloride in water. Liquid chlorine is made by putting the gas under pressure. Because chlorine is so poisonous, the equipment has to be carefully sealed.*

By the end of the 1990s, refrigerators will be manufactured without the use of chlorofluorocarbons. Many aerosol products are now produced without CFCs and alternative substances, such as hydrocarbons, carbon dioxide and nitrous oxide are now used to create the propellent forces.

Chlorine

Chlorine is a poisonous, yellowish-green GAS with an unpleasant smell. It causes irritation to the eyes, nose, throat and lungs. Chlorine is found in nature in COMPOUNDS called chlorides. The best known is sodium chloride (common salt). Chlorides are found in rock salt, in seawater and in salt lakes. Chlorine is made industrially by passing an electric current through a solution of sodium chloride; CAUSTIC SODA is also produced. The chlorine is collected and kept under PRESSURE as a liquid. Chlorine is used to kill bacteria in drinking water and in swimming pools. It is also a BLEACH and is used in the paper-making industry. Chlorine compounds are used in dyeing, and in making plastics, insecticides, disinfectants and cleaning fluids. Chlorine is one of the HALOGENS, or salt-producing non-metallic elements.

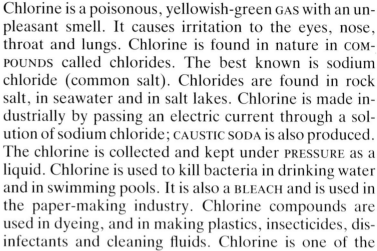

Chlorofluorocarbons (CFCs)

Chlorofluorocarbons, or CFCs, are chemical COMPOUNDS of CHLORINE, fluorine and CARBON. They are similar to HYDROCARBONS, but instead of HYDROGEN atoms being bonded to the carbon atoms, the carbon atoms are bonded to atoms of chlorine and fluorine (HALOGEN gases). CFCs have many industrial uses. They are used under pressure to propel AEROSOLS from cans. They are also used in refrigerators to help cooling agents circulate and are produced in the manufacture of PLASTIC foam for containers. CFCs are very stable over long

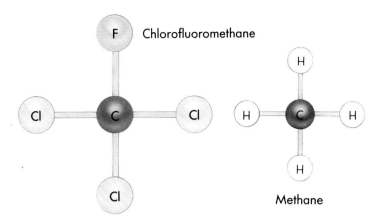

Chlorofluoromethane

H

H   C   H

H

Methane

◄ Chlorofluorocarbons have chlorine (Cl) and fluorine (F) atoms bonded to the carbon (C) atom instead of the hydrogen (H) atoms in hydrocarbons. Methane, the simplest hydrocarbon, can form chlorofluoromethane.

periods but eventually they give up their chlorine atoms and release them into the environment. Chlorine reacts with the OZONE LAYER in the atmosphere to form chlorine oxide. This reaction has begun to destroy the ozone layer. Conservationists fear that CFCs may destroy it altogether. Many countries no longer allow the use of CFCs and have signed international agreements to ban their use.

Chlorophyll

Chlorophyll is the PIGMENT in plant CELLS that gives them their green COLOUR. Most plant cells do not produce chlorophyll unless they are exposed to light. Chlorophyll is essential for PHOTOSYNTHESIS. It absorbs energy from the Sun's light and uses it to help the plants make food from carbon dioxide and water. Chlorophyll is a MOLECULE which is made up of mostly carbon and hydrogen, with a single atom of magnesium surrounded by nitrogen in its centre. It is contained in tiny chloroplasts which are located mainly in the LEAVES but may also occur in stems. In some leaves there are other pigments. In autumn, chlorophyll is not produced as much and the other pigments are more noticeable.

SEE FOR YOURSELF
Using a paper clip, fix a piece of paper to the edge of a large leaf. After a few days a pale patch will appear under the paper. This is because light is prevented from reaching the cells that make chlorophyll, the substance that makes plants green.

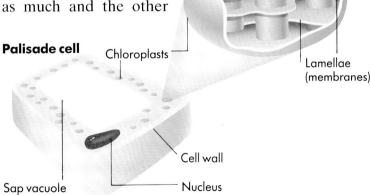

Granum

Lamellae (membranes)

▶ Chlorophyll is found in chloroplasts in the palisade cells in the leaves of plants. The pile of sheet-like membranes (or lamellae) inside the chloroplasts is called a granum. They hold the chlorophyll molecules and enzymes in the best position for trapping light energy from the Sun.

Palisade cell

Chloroplasts

Cell wall

Sap vacuole

Nucleus

117

Useful Cholesterol
Cholesterol and its by-products are secreted through the oil glands of the skin to act as a lubricant to soften the skin. It also provides a protective coating for the hair and skin. Sheep's wool, for example, is covered with a greasy coating containing lanolin, which is mainly made up of substances containing cholesterol.

Cholesterol

Cholesterol is a fatty material (a FAT or lipid) that exists in all animal tissues. The human body makes its own cholesterol but also takes in extra amounts of it in such foods as butter, eggs, fatty meats and liver. The membranes of CELLS contain cholesterol. It is used to make bile salts that help in digestion and to produce certain HORMONES. Most cholesterol is produced by the LIVER and is carried through the BLOOD to other cells by substances called lipoproteins. The presence of large amounts of certain types of cholesterol in the blood has been linked to certain diseases, for example arteriosclerosis (hardening of the arteries), which develops when fatty deposits due to cholesterol collect on the inner walls of arteries, making them narrow. Blood clots can block these narrow passages and cause a heart attack.

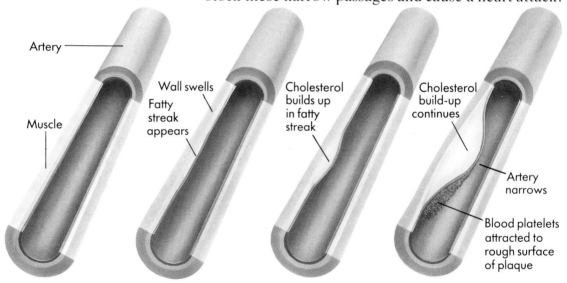

Artery

Muscle

Wall swells
Fatty streak appears

Cholesterol builds up in fatty streak

Cholesterol build-up continues

Artery narrows

Blood platelets attracted to rough surface of plaque

▲ Diseases such as arteriosclerosis (hardening of the arteries) develop when fat deposits, containing cholesterol, collect on the inner walls of the blood vessel forming a plaque. This causes the arteries to narrow. Blood clots can easily block these narrowed vessels. Heart attacks can result if the blockage occurs in the arteries close to the heart.

Chromatography

Chromatography is used to separate the different substances in a mixture of liquids or gases. It is an important technique used in chemical ANALYSIS. It is used to separate small amounts of substances, such as pollutants in air; to separate and measure the quantities of two or more substances produced by a CHEMICAL REACTION; and to remove impurities from substances. In *liquid column chromatography*, a tube is filled with absorbent material and a sample of the mixture is poured in at one end. Another liquid called an eluant is then poured in which

◀ *This machine analyses the chemical make-up of mixtures of gas and liquid samples. The samples are placed in numbered tubes. Results are given in the form of a chromatogram, a print-out of concentrations of the parts making up the mixture.*

SEE FOR YOURSELF
Tape 2 strips of blotting paper to a pencil. Hang the strips in a jar so that the end of each strip is in the water. Put a blob of different coloured washable ink on each strip above the level of the water. The paper absorbs the water and the different colours making up the blobs are dissolved at different speeds.

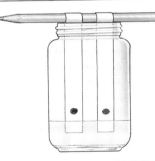

washes through the absorbent material. The different substances in the mixture are absorbed by the material at different rates as they are carried through by the eluant, each substance forming a distinct layer. *Thin layer chromatography* works in a similar way, except that the absorbent material is in the form of a thin film. In *gas chromatography*, used for analysing a gas mixture, helium is used as an eluant to carry the different gases in the mixture through a column of absorbent material.

Make 2 cuts in a circle of blotting paper and bend the strip into a jar of water. Put a blob of ink in the centre of the circle. As the water is absorbed by the paper it dissolves the ink. Rings of colour are formed as the ink is split into its parts.

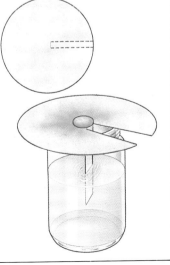

Chromium

Chromium is a hard bluish-white metallic ELEMENT that resists CORROSION and becomes shiny when polished. It occurs as chromite, which is a COMPOUND of chromium, iron and oxygen. Chromium was discovered in the late 1790s and now has a wide range of industrial uses. It is used to plate other metals, for example, on car bumpers. In the aircraft industry, its compounds are used to ANODIZE aluminium. Chromium, also often called

In 1913, Harry Brearley, a metals expert in Sheffield, England, was trying out some new steels when he noticed that all but a few pieces of steel in his scrapyard were badly rusted. He tested these pieces and found that they all contained chromium. This chance occurrence led to the vast stainless steel industry.

chrome, is added to steel to make it hard and corrosion-resistant. Steel containing more than 10 percent of chromium is called STAINLESS STEEL. Chromium compounds have distinctive colours and traces of these give rubies and emeralds their attractive red and green colours. Lead chromate and other compounds are used in paints and dyes. Chromium dioxide is used in magnetic recording tape.

► The black layer in this rock is the ore of chromium. Chromium is unusual as it only has one ore.

Thomas Hunt Morgan (1866–1945)
An American zoologist and geneticist, he won the Nobel Prize for Physiology in 1930 for his work linking chromosomes and heredity. His experiments with the fruit fly *Drosophila* showed that the genes, the units of heredity, were carried on the chromosomes. He later showed that the position of the genes on the chromosome controlled inherited characteristics.

Chromosomes and Genes

Inside the nucleus of every living CELL there are a number of microscopic threads called chromosomes. These chromosomes carry all the information necessary for the proper development of the cells and the whole body. They are the 'plans' from which the cells work. Each kind of plant or animal has its own particular number of

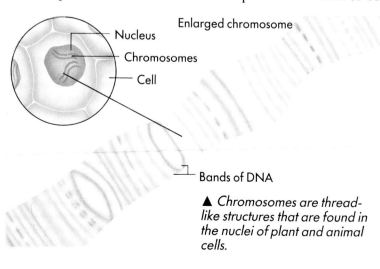

Enlarged chromosome
Nucleus
Chromosomes
Cell
Bands of DNA

▲ Chromosomes are thread-like structures that are found in the nuclei of plant and animal cells.

August Weismann (1834–1914)
Weismann was one of the founders of the science of genetics. He realized that something in the germ cells, contained in the sexual organs, was passed on to the next generation controlling their heredity. He found that inborn characteristics of both parents, such as height and eye colour, were combined in their offspring but that acquired characteristics were not inherited. He showed that offspring of mice which had had their tails cut off were born with normal tails.

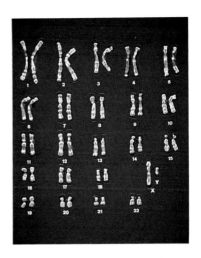

▲ Humans have 23 pairs of chromosomes in most of their cells. Males and females differ only in the sex chromosome of the 23rd pair. A female's chromosomes would look like XX, instead of XY.

chromosomes. They occur in pairs. Humans have 22 pairs in each normal cell plus two extra chromosomes, sex chromosomes, which decide the body's sex.

The chromosomes are made largely of chains of DNA molecules. Parts of these chains are genes, and there may be hundreds of them on a chromosome. Each one controls one or more features in the body by determining what PROTEINS are made in the cells. Proteins are the major materials of living cells.

Although we all have the same number of chromosomes in our cells, we have slightly different genes, and so we look different. When plants and animals reproduce, chromosomes and genes from both parents are mixed together.

See also CELL DIVISION; GENETICS; HEREDITY; NUCLEIC ACIDS.

Among plants many new species have arisen because the number of their chromosomes has changed. This occurs during cell division when the chromosomes fail to separate properly. Occasionally whole sets of chromosomes fail to separate; for example, the wheat used in bread flour has 42 chromosomes and its ancestors had 14 and 28 chromosomes.

Cinematography

Cinematography is film-making. A cinema FILM is actually a long strip of thousands of still photographs. The film strip is wound onto a spool, and the spool fitted to a projector. The film threads through the projector and each picture, or frame, is projected onto the screen. The pictures appear so rapidly (24 frames per second) that they merge together into smooth, lifelike movement. The images on the film are made by a special camera. It works like a still CAMERA, except that it takes 24 pictures every second on a continuous strip of film.

The first moving pictures or movies were made by the

Different genes
Organisms inherit two forms of the same gene for each characteristic. These forms may be identical or they may be different. If they are different then one form may be **dominant**, its effect will be seen in the organism, or it may be **recessive**, its effect will be hidden. Only if both forms of a gene, such as blue eye colour, are recessive will the organism show the recessive characteristic.

► *This explosion is one of the many stunning visual effects created for the film* Indiana Jones and the Last Crusade.

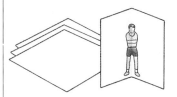

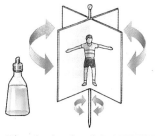

inventor, Thomas Alva EDISON. They were shown in a machine called a Kinetoscope. However, only one person at a time could see the film. The French Lumière brothers were the first to make a cinema projector that allowed a number of people to see the film together.

The earliest movies were silent. Sound recording had been invented but there was not yet a successful way of keeping the sound in step with the pictures, called synchronization. The first Hollywood movie with synchronized sound, a 'talkie', was *The Jazz Singer*, starring Al Jolson, shown for the first time in the United States in 1927. Colour film only became available in the 1930s. Most films have been made in colour since the 1950s. *See also* PHOTOGRAPHY.

Circuit breaker

A circuit breaker is a device that stops an electric CIRCUIT working in the event of an abnormal or dangerous situation. A sudden increase in the electric current can damage electrical equipment or start a fire. Most electrical equipment in the home and office and its users are protected from dangerous electrical faults by FUSES. In a fuse, a thin wire heats up and melts, cutting off the power supply. A new fuse must be fitted before the equipment will work again. Modern circuit breakers use ELECTRONIC sensors to detect faults and switch the power off. The power can be switched on again by pressing a switch on the circuit breaker to reset it.

Circuit, electric

An electric circuit is a loop of electrical CONDUCTORS through which an electric current of ELECTRONS can flow. You can think of a current like a flow of water; in just the same way as water can be pumped round a circuit of pipes and made to drive water wheels, an electric current is driven round the circuit and made to light bulbs or run motors. The electrical equivalent of a pump is the BATTERY, which uses chemical ENERGY stored within it to drive the electric current. Just as the pump has to overcome friction to force water through the pipes, the battery has to overcome electrical RESISTANCE to make a current flow in the circuit. If the current has to flow through several resistances (light bulbs can be used as resistances), one after the other, then the battery is not able to make so much current flow; the resistances are said to be in series. If the resistances are arranged so that some of the current flows through one and some through another, they are said to be in parallel.

Circuits with batteries work with direct current; the flow of current is always in the same direction. Most mechanical GENERATORS generate an alternating current which flows alternately in opposite directions. The electric sockets in houses are connected through large electrical circuits to the generators in power stations, and carry an alternating current.

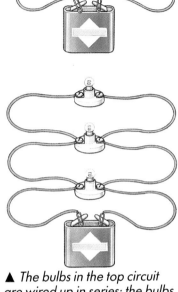

▲ The bulbs in the top circuit are wired up in series; the bulbs are all sharing the power so they are dim. The bulbs in the bottom circuit are wired up in parallel; each bulb has its own connection to the battery and so is not dim.

SEE FOR YOURSELF
Fold a piece of card, about 15 cm by 2 cm. Tape 2 strips of tin foil round the card, and a wire to each. Join the wires to a circuit with a battery and a bulb in it. When the card is stepped on, the 2 pieces of foil press together making a circuit, and the bulb lights up.

Foil
Tape
Card

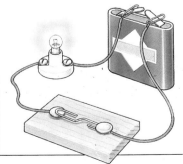

Make a switch by pressing 2 drawing pins into a piece of wood and connecting them to the circuit with wires. Hook one end of a paper clip round a drawing pin and use the other end to close the circuit by pressing it down on the other drawing pin.

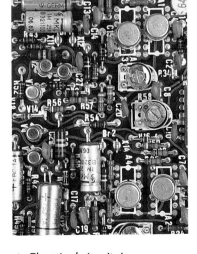

▲ Electrical circuits in appliances are made up of different components, attached to a circuit board.

William Harvey (1578–1657)
Harvey was an English physician. He was the first to accurately describe the circulation of the blood. He showed that blood moves around the body in only one direction along arteries and veins.

Circulation

Circulation is the process in which BLOOD is moved around an organism's body by the HEART so that cells and organs in every part of the body can receive oxygen and food substances from the blood, and waste materials can be carried away. Blood also contains chemical messengers called HORMONES which can activate or switch off certain body processes as required. Humans have a double circulation. Blood leaving the right side of the heart is pumped through the LUNGS, where it picks up oxygen and releases carbon dioxide and water vapour. This oxygenated blood then returns to the left side of the heart, and is pumped round the body until it comes back again to the right side of the heart. Blood always leaves the heart through arteries, passes through microscopically small capillaries, then returns along veins.

▶ The blood is pumped from the heart into arteries and circulates through veins back to the heart.

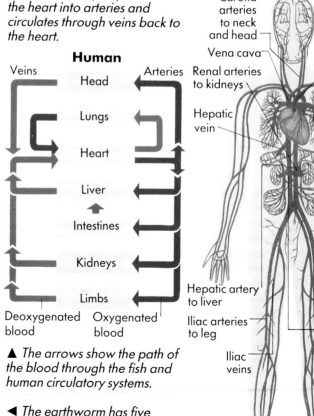

Fish

Human

Gills
Heart
Liver
Gut
Kidneys
Tail

Veins · Head · Arteries
Lungs
Heart
Liver
Intestines
Kidneys
Limbs

Deoxygenated blood   Oxygenated blood

▲ The arrows show the path of the blood through the fish and human circulatory systems.

Carotid arteries to neck and head
Vena cava
Pulmonary arteries to lung
Aorta
Renal arteries to kidneys
Hepatic vein
Hepatic artery to liver
Iliac arteries to leg
Pulmonary vein
Renal vein
Iliac veins

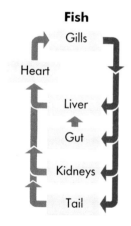

Shell
Lung
Snail
Heart
Sinus

◀ The earthworm has five hearts to circulate its blood. In snails, blood flows from vessels into open spaces between organs. It moves through these spaces to return to the heart.

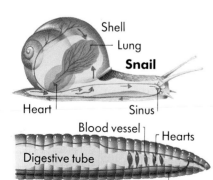

Blood vessel
Hearts
Digestive tube
Earthworm   Nerve cord

CLASSIFICATION

There are over a million kinds of animals and nearly half a million kinds of plants, so it is essential to have some way of classifying them or arranging them into groups so that we can refer to them easily. Look at the plants and animals around you and you will probably see several ways of classifying them. You might decide to group the flowers according to their colours. This is an easy way to do it, but it is not a very satisfactory way because it would put red and white tulips in separate groups when they clearly belong together. Classifying by colour is an artificial classification and it tells us nothing about the structure or the biology of the flowers. Biologists use natural systems of classification, in which the members of each group have similar structures and are related to each other.

In the present day classification system, species of animals that are closely related are grouped into a genus (plural genera). Genera with similar characteristics are grouped into families. Families, in turn, are grouped into orders; orders into classes; and classes into phyla. Finally, related phyla are placed into kingdoms. Plants are classified in the same way, although the major groups are often called divisions instead of phyla. Aristotle was one of the first people to attempt to classify animals and plants in this way, but the Swedish naturalist Linnaeus laid the foundations of modern classification in the 18th century.

SEE FOR YOURSELF

Find some small animals and make some drawings of them. Notice how their legs and other parts are arranged. This is how scientists classify animals. Those with parts arranged in the same way are generally closely related.

Grasshopper

Spider

Ladybird

Centipede

Earwig

Woodlouse

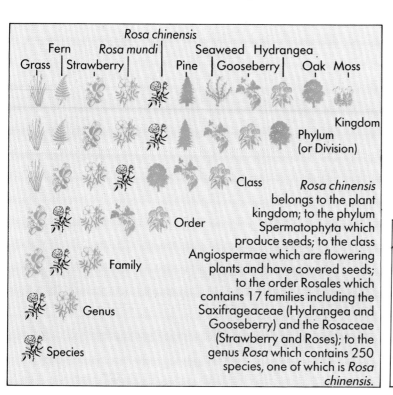

Rosa chinensis

Fern | Rosa mundi | Seaweed | Hydrangea
Grass | Strawberry | Pine | Gooseberry | Oak | Moss

Kingdom

Phylum (or Division)

Class

Order

Family

Genus

Species

Rosa chinensis belongs to the plant kingdom; to the phylum Spermatophyta which produce seeds; to the class Angiospermae which are flowering plants and have covered seeds; to the order Rosales which contains 17 families including the Saxifrageaceae (Hydrangea and Gooseberry) and the Rosaceae (Strawberry and Roses); to the genus *Rosa* which contains 250 species, one of which is *Rosa chinensis*.

▶ Organisms are named using a binomial (two name) system introduced by Linnaeus. The first name is the genus and the second, the species name. Even the common housefly is named like this — *Musca domestica*.

◀ Different levels of classification of the plant kingdom showing how one plant species *Rosa chinensis* can be separated from other plants.

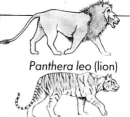

Panthera leo (lion)

Panthera tigris (tiger)
These two cats belong to the same genus, *Panthera*, but, different species.

See also BIOLOGY; BOTANY; LINNAEUS; MICROBIOLOGY; MICROORGANISMS; ZOOLOGY.

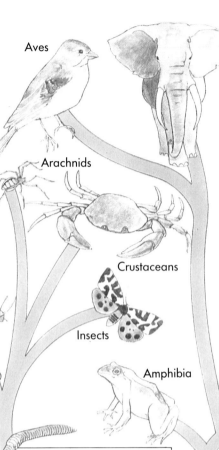

The **Arthropoda** is the largest animal phylum, and includes arachnids, crustaceans and insects among others. They have an external skeleton and jointed appendages.

The **Mollusca** is the second-largest phylum. They are soft-bodied animals and most have a shell to protect them. They include snails, bivalves and octopuses.

Snails

Octopuses

Bivalves

The phylum **Annelida** are limbless animals whose soft bodies are divided into segments. They include the earthworms and their relatives.

Annelida

The phylum **Coelenterata** are a group of soft-bodied animals, most of which live in the sea. They include jellyfishes, sea anemones and corals.

Coelenterata

Sponges

Protozoa

The phylum **Protozoa** contains microscopic animals, each consisting of only a single cell. There are more than 30,000 different kinds of protozoa.

Mammalia

Aves

Arachnids

Crustaceans

Insects

Amphibia

Reptilia

The class **Mammalia** contains the mammals. They are warm-blooded animals with hair. Offspring are fed on milk from the mother.

The class **Aves** contains the birds, separated from all other animals by their feathers. All birds hatch from eggs and have wings but not all can fly.

The class **Reptilia** contains the reptiles, which are scaly, cold-blooded animals and include lizards, snakes, crocodiles and tortoises.

The class **Amphibia** contains cold-blooded animals that spend part of their lives in water and part on land. They include frogs, toads and newts.

Fishes belong to several classes in the phylum **Chordata**. They all live in water, swim with fins and almost all breathe through gills.

Echinoderms

Fishes

THE ANIMAL KINGDOM
The animal kingdom is divided into about 30 major groups. Animals with one or more of the same body characteristics are separated into major groups called phyla. Animals with backbones, called vertebrates, plus a few other creatures belong to the phylum Chordata. They include the lancelets, fish, amphibians, reptiles, birds and mammals. All the other phyla contain more than 950,000 species of animals without backbones, called invertebrates. Amongst these phyla are the annelids, molluscs, arthropods and the echinoderms (starfishes and sea urchins). Not all scientists agree about the number of phyla as some animals do not fit tidily into phyla. The velvet worms, for example, are neither annelids nor arthropods and so can be put into a phylum of their own.

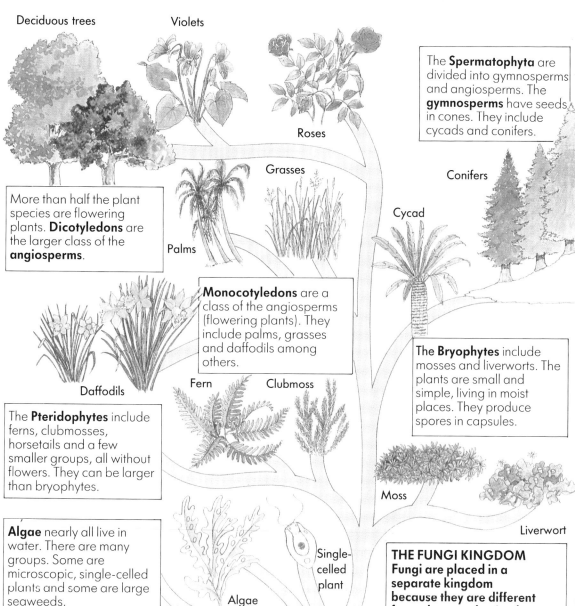

Deciduous trees

Violets

Roses

Grasses

The Spermatophyta are divided into gymnosperms and angiosperms. The **gymnosperms** have seeds in cones. They include cycads and conifers.

Conifers

Cycad

More than half the plant species are flowering plants. **Dicotyledons** are the larger class of the **angiosperms**.

Palms

Monocotyledons are a class of the angiosperms (flowering plants). They include palms, grasses and daffodils among others.

The Bryophytes include mosses and liverworts. The plants are small and simple, living in moist places. They produce spores in capsules.

Daffodils

Fern

Clubmoss

The **Pteridophytes** include ferns, clubmosses, horsetails and a few smaller groups, all without flowers. They can be larger than bryophytes.

Moss

Liverwort

Algae nearly all live in water. There are many groups. Some are microscopic, single-celled plants and some are large seaweeds.

Single-celled plant

Algae

THE FUNGI KINGDOM
Fungi are placed in a separate kingdom because they are different from plants and animals. They include toadstools, yeasts and moulds. They live almost anywhere in the soil, water and air. They do not produce their own food, since they have no chlorophyll, so they take nutrients from the animals, plants or decaying matter on which they live. They reproduce by spores sexually or asexually.

THE PLANT KINGDOM
Several systems are used to classify the 450,000 or so kinds of plants that belong to the plant kingdom. The main divisions, or phyla, of the plant kingdom are the Algae, Bryophyta, Pteriodophyta and the Spermatophyta. The spermatophytes make up the largest phylum, consisting of over 350,000 different species which reproduce by way of seeds. There are two kinds of seed-bearing plants, the gymnosperms, or 'naked seed' plants, and the angiosperms, or 'covered seed' plants. The angiosperms, which include all of the flowering plants, are divided into two classes, the monocotyledons, plants with one seedleaf, and the dicotyledons, plants with two seedleaves. The other phyla do not produce flowers and all reproduce by scattering particles called spores.

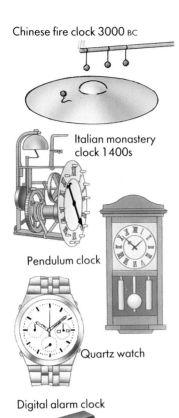

Chinese fire clock 3000 BC

Italian monastery clock 1400s

Pendulum clock

Quartz watch

Digital alarm clock

Mechanical watch

▲ *There have been ways of measuring time for many thousands of years. At first clocks were only accurate to the nearest hour but now they can measure seconds precisely.*

▶ *Mechanical watches and some small mechanical clocks are regulated by a balance wheel and spring. The wheel spins one way and then the other. It makes an arm rock to and fro which allows the escape wheel to move round one step at a time. The escape wheel is driven by the clock's mainspring, which slowly unwinds.*

Climate

The climate of a particular region of the world describes the average WEATHER conditions over a long period of time, at least 50 years. These conditions include the average TEMPERATURE, rainfall, air PRESSURE, HUMIDITY, hours of sunshine, and wind speed and direction in that region. *See* pages 132 and 133.

Clocks and Watches

Clocks and watches are designed to show the passage of TIME. Clocks usually stand on their own and watches are strapped to the wrist. Time was probably first measured several thousand years ago by observing the position of the Sun in the sky. Water clocks and sandglasses, or hour glasses, used changing levels of water or sand in a container to measure time. Candles burn at a constant rate and can be used to measure time. Sundials use the movement of shadows cast by the Sun. The first mechanical timepieces were made in China in the 8th century.

All mechanical timepieces need a source of power. Before electric power, clocks used springs or weights. Many modern clocks and watches are powered by batteries. Digital watches have no moving parts. Instead of hands, the time is shown by numbers on a tiny screen. *See also* LIQUID CRYSTAL DISPLAY; MEASUREMENT.

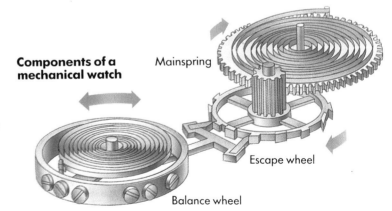

Components of a mechanical watch

Mainspring

Escape wheel

Balance wheel

Clones

Clones are living creatures reproduced or copied from a single CELL, without sexual REPRODUCTION or meiosis taking place. This means that the new organisms are physically and genetically identical to the 'parent' cell. Identical twins are produced naturally in this way, when the EGG cell splits after FERTILIZATION and separates into two separate EMBRYOS, sharing identical genes. It is possible to produce cloned animals in the laboratory.

Cloning is a commercial process often used in plant BREEDING, where flowers or crop plants are produced in huge numbers from a single cell taken from a plant with the desired characteristics. This process results in a population with identical genes, and this is not always good; in the case of plants, some varieties with useful properties could die out without passing on their genes.

Closed circuit television *See* Television

Cloud

A cloud is a mass of tiny droplets of water floating in the AIR sometimes at a great distance from the Earth's surface. Water VAPOUR is water in the form of a GAS and, under normal conditions, it is invisible. If you boil a kettle, for example, the water vapour which is produced cannot be seen at first. It is only when the vapour cools and condenses into drops of LIQUID water that you see the steam.

All air contains water vapour from EVAPORATION of lakes, ponds, rivers and seas. Almost 500 million tonnes of water pass between the Earth and the air every year.

Warm air can hold more water vapour than cool air before the water condenses. As air rises, it becomes

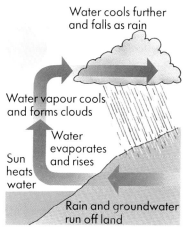

▲ Clouds are formed from water that has evaporated from oceans, rivers, lakes, or from moist soil and plants. The evaporated water cools as it rises. When it has cooled enough, the vapour condenses and forms clouds.

Cirrus

Cirrostratus

Altocumulus

Cirrocumulus

Altostratus

Cumulus

Stratocumulus

Stratus

Nimbostratus

Cumulonimbus

'Mother of pearl' clouds are not often seen. When they do occur they appear at great height and provide one of the most beautiful displays in the sky. They have a rainbow-coloured marbled texture, which is continually changing.

◀ Different types of clouds are seen at various heights above the Earth. Clouds that appear as layers or sheets are called stratus clouds. Those that appear as piled up white masses are known as cumulus clouds, and high, wispy clouds are called cirrus clouds.

Despite the fact that coal is not as important as it was, coal-burning power plants still produce almost two-thirds of the world's electricity.

cooler so that, eventually, the air becomes saturated with water vapour. If the saturated air continues to rise and cool, the water vapour condenses into drops of liquid water. If the cloud gets even colder the drops of CONDENSATION become large enough to form rain. These are the clouds you see in the sky. If a mass of air falls, however, it gets warmer and so holds more water vapour. There are different clouds defined and named after their shape and height in the ATMOSPHERE.

Coal

Coal is a black or blackish rock, consisting chiefly of CARBON. There are two main kinds, anthracite or hard coal, and bituminous or soft coal. It is one of the main FOSSIL FUELS, formed during the Carboniferous period (about 350–250 million years ago) from the rotting vegetation of tropical forests. This became overlaid by other rocks and gradually turned into coal. Most coal is found in bands or seams at varying depths under the ground. When we burn it we are releasing the Sun's ENERGY, stored for millions of years in the partly fossilized vegetable matter.

Coal was the most important fuel of the INDUSTRIAL REVOLUTION and also the chief domestic FUEL. In the last 50 years, coal has largely been replaced by other fossil fuels. But many of its by-products are still used in detergents, antiseptics, dyes, pesticides and medical drugs.

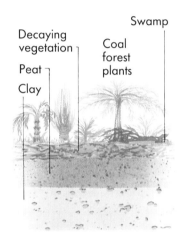

▲ The remains of dead plants in prehistoric forests became peat which was gradually buried and subjected to great pressure. After many thousands of years the peat turned into coal.

▶ Coal deposits deeper than 60 m are normally mined underground. Shaft mines have access passages which run straight down from the surface to the coal seam. The coal is taken to the surface using a hoist.

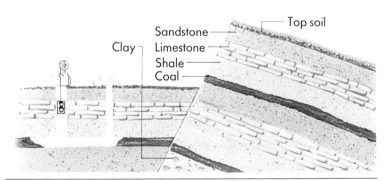

Cockerell, Christopher *See* Hovercraft

Cold

Something is cold when its TEMPERATURE is lower than its surroundings. Things that feel cold to us have a temperature lower than our body temperature. When objects are cold, the MOLECULES in them are moving around more slowly than in hotter objects. The molecules in hotter objects tend to bump into the molecules in a colder one causing the cold object to heat up. For this reason it is difficult to keep an object very much colder than its surroundings.

Cryogenics is the study of low temperatures and their effects. It has helped scientists to perform experiments at only a few millionths of a degree above absolute zero, which is as cold as it is possible to get since all molecules would stop moving at absolute zero.

See also CONDUCTION, HEAT; EVAPORATION; HEAT.

Colloids

A colloid is halfway between a SOLUTION and a SUSPENSION. In a colloid, particles of MATTER measuring between about one-millionth of a millimetre and one-tenth of a millimetre in diameter are evenly scattered throughout liquid or gas.

Smoke is a colloid in which microscopic solid particles are dispersed in the air. This kind of colloid is also known as an AEROSOL. Other colloids include dairy products like butter, the cytoplasm of CELLS, and fluids found inside our body tissues. An EMULSION is a colloid in which droplets of a liquid are scattered evenly in another liquid. In a FOAM, a gas (usually air) is dispersed in a liquid. A paste is a concentrated mixture in which solid particles are dispersed in a liquid. An example of a typical paste is toothpaste.

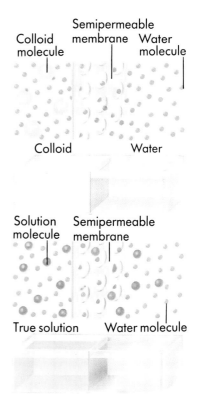

▲ The particles in a colloid, such as cream, are larger than those of a true solution, such as food colouring and water. The colloid particles cannot diffuse through a membrane into the water on the other side of the container, but the particles of true solution can, turning the clear water pink.

◄ Milk is a colloidal dispersion of fats in water. During cheese-making the milk is separated into curds (the solid milk fats lumped together) and whey (the liquid). The curd is then packed into moulds for pressing into cheese.

CLIMATE

Temperature and rainfall are the most important factors determining the climate. If you look at a map of the world's climates or even at separate maps of average rainfall and temperature, you can see that there is a rough pattern. The different climates seem to occupy bands running horizontally across a map with North at the top and South at the bottom. There is another factor which affects climate; the distribution of land and sea. This is because continental areas heat up and cool down more quickly than the sea which tends to have a moderating effect on the weather pattern of an area.

Warm air holds far more water than cold air. Close to the equator, air is warmed by the Sun and holds a lot of water evaporated from the oceans. As it rises, the water condenses into clouds and falls as rain so this area tends to be hot and wet. Further North or South at the tropics, the air which has risen and circulated from the equatorial area is falling again. As the air falls it warms up so it can hold more water at the tropics. Here, the world's hot, dry deserts occur because there is very little rain.

The Sun's rays heat the atmosphere only a little. It is the heat reflected back from the Earth that has the most warming effect. In the polar regions, the Sun's rays must travel much further through the air before reaching the ground and they lose a lot of the Sun's warmth on the way. The air is so cold at the poles that what water there is falls as snow. These are the coldest parts of the world. The climate of areas between these three main climatic zones tends to be more variable, and the presence of mountains, forests or large cities can affect it.

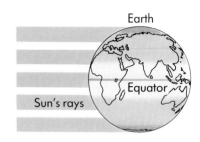

Earth

Equator

Sun's rays

▲ *Every place on Earth has its own climate. Regions near the equator, where the Sun shines directly overhead, have a hotter climate than those further away.*

▼ *The Earth can be roughly divided into six climatic zones. Within each zone there are variations due to altitude and latitude.*

Polar climate

Mountain climate

Cold forest climate

Mid-latitude (temperate) climate

Dry (desert) climate

Tropical rainy climate

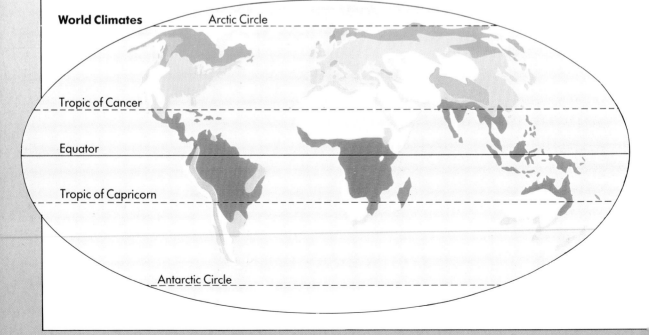

World Climates

Arctic Circle

Tropic of Cancer

Equator

Tropic of Capricorn

Antarctic Circle

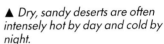

▲ *Dry, sandy deserts are often intensely hot by day and cold by night.*

◀ *A freezing desert, the Antarctic, has the most severe climate in the world.*

Climatic Zones

Polar climate: Always cold (average temperature below 10°C), brief chilly summer, little precipitation.
Mountain climate: Affected by altitude, cooler and wetter than the climates of neighbouring areas.
Cold forest climate: (also called subarctic) Short, cool summer (four months at 10°C to 20°C) and long, cold winter, light to moderate precipitation.
Mid-latitude (temperate) climate: Moderately warm summer and mild, cool winter (eight months, average temperature 10°C to 20°C), moderate precipitation in all seasons.
Dry (desert) climate: Hot to cold, great changes in daily temperature except in coastal areas, little precipitation.
Tropical rainy climate: Always hot and wet (temperatures above 20°C), heavy precipitation throughout the year.

SEE FOR YOURSELF

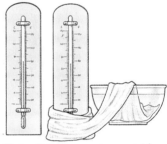

Place 2 thermometers outside. Wrap a damp cloth round the bulb of one thermometer and put the end into a bowl of water. When humidity is low the difference between the 2 thermometer readings will be greater than when humidity is high, because water from the damp cloth evaporates quickly and cools the thermometer.

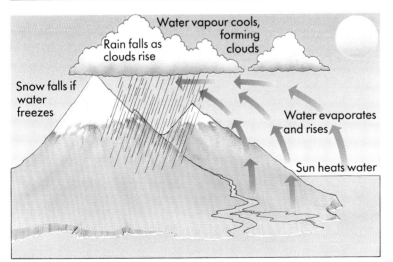

Water vapour cools, forming clouds

Rain falls as clouds rise

Snow falls if water freezes

Water evaporates and rises

Sun heats water

◀ *The Sun heats the surface of the sea. Hot air containing water vapour rises rapidly. As it rises the air cools and the vapour condenses to form water droplets, which develop into clouds. The droplets fall to the Earth as rain. If the water droplets freeze they fall as snow.*

See also CELSIUS; CLOUD; CYCLONE; DESERT; EVAPORATION; FRONT, WEATHER; HEAT; METEOROLOGY; PRECIPITATION; SUN; TEMPERATURE; WEATHER; WIND.

COLOUR ⚛

Light is a wave, a form of electromagnetic radiation. Different colours are made up of light with different wavelengths. The longest wavelength of light that we can see is red light and the shortest wavelength is blue light. Different substances in the world around us give off light of different colours because they are different chemically, and it seems that animals have evolved the ability to see various colours to help them tell these different substances apart.

There are special cells in your eye, called cones because of their shape, which can distinguish light of different colours when it falls on them. Some animals, such as dogs, do not have any cones in their eyes so we believe that they do not have colour vision. The cones work well only in quite strong light, so in the dark everything looks the same colour.

Some animals which are active at night (owls, for example) have developed the ability to see light with wavelengths longer than those of red light. Similarly some insects such as bees can distinguish markings on flowers that give off ultraviolet light. This has a shorter wavelength than the blue we can see.

Light with a shorter wavelength carries more energy than light with a longer one. When an object gives out heat by radiation, the wavelength of the light becomes shorter as the object becomes hotter so it glows first red, then white, then blue. Astronomers use the colour of the light from the Sun and from other stars to find out their temperatures.

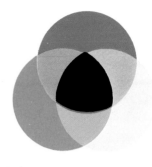

▲ When mixing pigments, the primary colours are yellow, blue and red.

▲ When mixing lights, the primary colours are red, green and blue. All three together make white light.

	Ultraviolet	Visible spectrum	Infrared
Cats and dogs	Bees	Humans	Owls

▲ Not all animals can see light from the same part of the spectrum.

SEE FOR YOURSELF

Try mixing coloured lights. Use 3 torches covered with red, green and blue see-through plastic. Green and red mix to make yellow; blue and green to make turquoise, and red and blue to make purple.

Spin a disc painted with the colours of the spectrum. As the disc spins you see white as the different colours merge together.

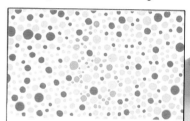

Colour-blindness is the inability to tell some colours apart. If you have normal colour vision you should see the number 6.

White light can be split into the colours of the spectrum using a prism. The colours it is made up of are red, orange, yellow, green, blue, indigo and violet. A rainbow is a spectrum of light.

See also CAMOUFLAGE; ELECTROMAGNETIC PRISM; RAINBOW; SPECTRUM; RADIATION; EYE; LIGHT; WAVELENGTH.

Combustion

Combustion is a chemical process in which substances react together in a fast CHEMICAL REACTION accompanied by HEAT and LIGHT in the form of a BURNING flame. Combustion may also be accompanied by an EXPLOSION. In combustion, one of the reacting substances is usually the gas OXYGEN, and chemists commonly use the term combustion to mean the rapid OXIDATION of a substance through burning. However, the burning in other gases (for example, hydrogen in chlorine) may also be referred to as combustion. The speed of a combustion reaction determines the temperature of a burning substance, but the total amount of heat given out by the burning substance during the reaction is always the same, whether the substance burns quickly or slowly. There are many industrial applications of combustion and, of course, in the INTERNAL COMBUSTION ENGINE.

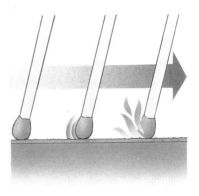

▲ A match is struck against the rough surface of the side of the matchbox. This makes the head of the match get hot and the match lights because the head contains substances that combust when they get hot.

◀ The temperature in the combustion chamber of a solid-propellant rocket, such as those used to launch the Space Shuttle, ranges from 1600°C to 3300°C.

Some substances can burst into flames without anything being done to set them alight. This is called spontaneous combustion and is caused by slow oxidation. Damp coal sometimes begins to burn without being ignited. The same thing can happen to piles of oily rags.

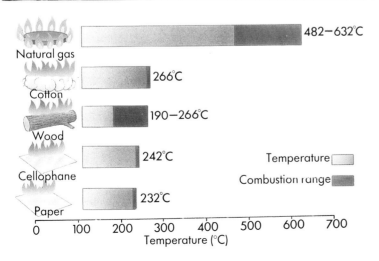

Natural gas — 482–632°C

Cotton — 266°C

Wood — 190–266°C

Cellophane — 242°C

Paper — 232°C

Temperature

Combustion range

Temperature (°C)

◀ Every burnable substance has a particular temperature to which it must be heated before it combusts. The lower the temperature, the more easily the substance will catch fire. Some substances will burn at a range of temperatures.

135

The closest approach to Halley's comet occurred in 1986. It was by the European Space Agency's Giotto spacecraft, which came to within 539 km of the comet's core before its cameras stopped working because of the dust. Giotto revealed that the comet's core is a very black peanut-shaped body about 15 by 4 km in size.

Comet

A comet is a member of the SOLAR SYSTEM, orbiting the SUN. The solid part of a comet, the nucleus, is very small (a few kilometres across) but the cloud of gas and dust boiling away from the nucleus, the tail, can stretch out millions of kilometres. Comets are believed to be left-over particles from the beginning of the Solar System, when most of these particles collided with each other to build up the planets. The comet nuclei, containing

▶ Particles of gas and dust are swept outwards into a tail behind a comet as it approaches the Sun. When a comet moves away from the Sun, its tail leads.

▼ Comets are not normally seen until they are within the orbit of Jupiter. By then the Sun has melted some of the ice they contain. Gases and dust are given off which reflect light well and make the comets more visible.

crumbly rock particles trapped in frozen liquid, were left. If their orbits take them near the Sun, the heat turns the outer ice to vapour and the solid particles are released as dust. In their frozen state far from the Sun, comets are invisible. Each time a comet passes near the Sun it pours some more of its nucleus into space. Eventually it 'dies' and becomes just an orbiting rock.

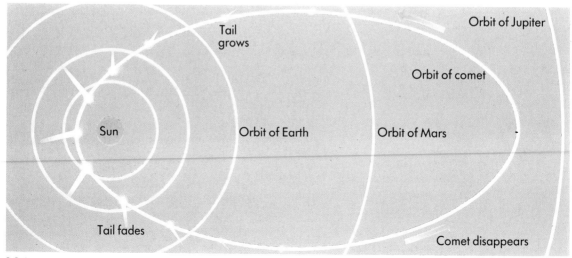

Tail grows

Orbit of Jupiter

Orbit of comet

Sun

Orbit of Earth

Orbit of Mars

Tail fades

Comet disappears

COMMUNICATIONS ⚙

Communication means exchanging ideas and information between organisms. For example, a dog warns another dog not to come closer by showing its teeth and snarling. Some moths find a mate by releasing a chemical that other moths can detect. Humans have developed language and then writing. This enables us to express complicated ideas and information.

Technology has given us new ways of communicating. Telecommunications give us almost instant communication with people and machines long distances apart. Computers can exchange information automatically through the telephone. Newspapers, radios, television and the cinema enable information to be communicated to millions of people.

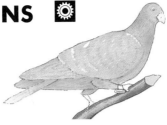

▲ Carrier pigeons are bred specially to carry messages over long distances. The message is tucked under a ring attached to one of its legs.

▲ Around 5000 years ago, pictorial messages were inscribed on stone, leading to writing.

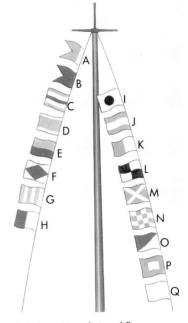

▲ International signal flags are used by ships at sea. Each flag represents a letter of the alphabet and has an internationally recognized meaning.

▲ A fax machine enables people to send letters and documents to each other within a matter of seconds.

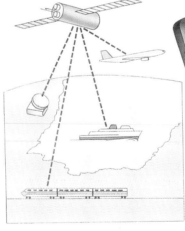

▲ Communications satellites are used to transmit and relay information around the world.

▲ In the future, everybody may have a compact telephone.

SEE FOR YOURSELF
Make your own telephone. Push the ends of a piece of string through 2 paper cups, knot the

ends and pull tight. When you speak into 1 cup, the sound waves travel along the string.

See also BEHAVIOUR; CELLULAR RADIO AND TELEPHONES; COMPUTER; RADIO; TECHNOLOGY; TELECOMMUNICATIONS; TELEGRAPH; TELEPHONE; TELEVISION.

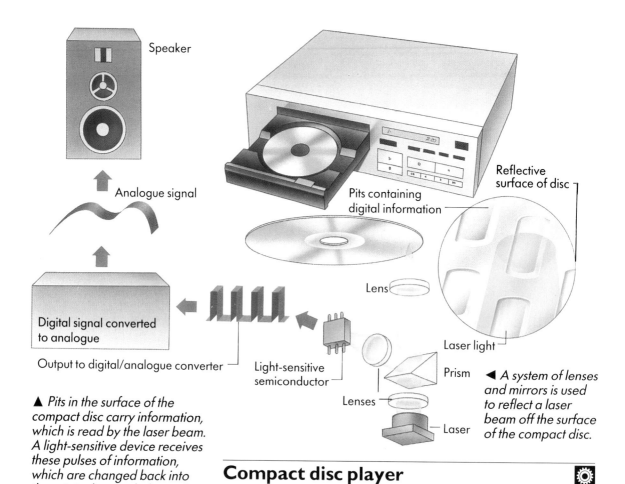

Speaker

Analogue signal

Digital signal converted to analogue

Output to digital/analogue converter

Light-sensitive semiconductor

Lenses

Laser

Prism

Laser light

Lens

Pits containing digital information

Reflective surface of disc

▲ *Pits in the surface of the compact disc carry information, which is read by the laser beam. A light-sensitive device receives these pulses of information, which are changed back into the original, recorded sound.*

◀ *A system of lenses and mirrors is used to reflect a laser beam off the surface of the compact disc.*

The laser beam in a compact disc player must be very fine to read only one track of the disc at a time. The tracks are only 1.6 micrometres (millionths of a metre) apart. The pits are only 0.5 micrometres wide and 1 to 3 micrometres long. The laser produces an intense, but invisible, infrared beam measuring only 1 micrometre across at its focus.

Compact disc player

A compact disc player is a machine used to play music recorded on a special type of disc. Unlike a vinyl record, a compact disc has no grooves. Music is recorded on the disc as tiny pits etched into a layer of ALUMINIUM. The aluminium is protected by sealing it inside a clear layer of smooth PLASTIC. The music on the disc is played by directing a LASER beam onto the disc. The beam is reflected back to a detector by the smooth aluminium, but not by the rough surface of the pits. As the disc spins at high speed and the laser beam scans across the disc surface, the detector produces a series of pulses representing the pattern of pits etched into the disc. The player's electronic circuits change the pulses back into a copy of the original music.

The speed of the disc varies. When the laser is reading tracks near the centre, the disc spins at its maximum speed, 500 revolutions per minute (rpm). As the laser moves to the edge, the speed reduces to 200 rpm so that information is read at a constant rate. The laser never actually touches the disc, so it should not wear out.

Compass

A compass points in a particular direction on the EARTH's surface; usually it shows North. The earliest and most common kind of compass, first used by Chinese sailors around AD 1100, worked by detecting the magnetism produced within the Earth. If a metal needle is magnetized and suspended so that it is free to turn it will point on a line which runs approximately North to South. The Earth's magnetic field changes with time, and so does the direction of this 'magnetic north'.

Other types of compass which do not use the Earth's magnetic field are now in use, including the GYROCOMPASS and inertial navigation systems which use LASERS.

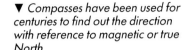

▼ Compasses have been used for centuries to find out the direction with reference to magnetic or true North.

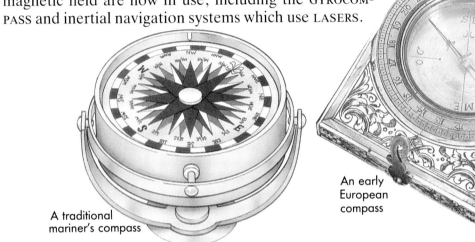

A traditional mariner's compass

An early European compass

SEE FOR YOURSELF
Place a small piece of cork in the centre of a saucer of water. Magnetize a steel needle by running a magnet along it from the eye to the point. Carefully place the needle on top of the cork. The needle and cork will spin round to point to magnetic North. Magnetic North is actually 1600 km from the geographic North Pole.

Compound

A chemical compound is a substance consisting of ATOMS of two or more different ELEMENTS, held together in identical MOLECULES by means of chemical BONDS. In water, two parts of hydrogen combine with one part of oxygen. So one molecule of water contains two atoms of

▲ Most elements do not exist on their own but as compounds with other elements. The colours visible in this rock are compounds of iron and niobium. Niobium is a rare metal which is often used with steel to make alloys that are resistant to high temperatures.

There are millions of compounds. The atoms of carbon and hydrogen alone join in different ways to make thousands of compounds. For example, they combine to form methane (CH_4), the main component of natural gas. They also combine to form propane (C_3H_8) which is the fuel used for camping stoves.

▶ This industrial compressor uses compressed air to power heavy-duty construction tools. Compressors are used for jobs, such as breaking up concrete or paving, drilling, pile driving, sand-blasting and tunnelling. A compressor works on the same principle as a pump. A piston moves backwards and forwards inside a hollow cylinder, which compresses the air and forces it into a hollow chamber. A pipe or hose connected to the chamber channels the compressed air to the tools.

hydrogen and one of oxygen. This relationship, discovered by Sir John Dalton (1766–1844), enables chemists to write down formulae in CHEMICAL SYMBOLS that show the composition of a compound. The formula for water is H_2O. There is a huge number of both natural and artificial compounds. Apart from water, the most familiar compounds include salt (sodium and chlorine, NaCl) and sugar (carbon, hydrogen and oxygen, $C_6H_{12}O_6$). Compounds are different from MIXTURES because in a mixture the atoms of the different elements do not combine chemically and are not present in fixed proportions. Elements in a mixture can usually be separated easily; those in a compound cannot.

See also CHEMISTRY; POLYMER; SALTS, CHEMICAL.

Compressor

A compressor is a machine used to increase the PRESSURE of AIR above its normal or atmospheric pressure. Compressed air is used in a wide range of activities. The outside of buildings are often cleaned by ABRASIVES in a process called sand-blasting where sand, in a jet of air from a compressor, strips away the surface layer of dirt coating the stone. Compressors are used to fill with compressed air the tanks that underwater divers need.

A variety of tools can be powered by compressed air. The drills used to dig holes through concrete and roads are powered by air from large compressors. All sorts of vehicles are painted, not with brushes, but by spraying the paint onto the metalwork. The jet of air that carries the paint from the spray-gun to the vehicle is provided by a compressor.

See also PNEUMATICS.

Computer

A computer is a machine that processes information (data), at great speed according to a set of instructions (a computer program). Different programs in various COM-PUTER LANGUAGES are used to process data in different ways, though the computer is performing the same simple operations. *See* pages 142 and 143.

Computer graphics

Computer graphics are pictures produced by a COM-PUTER. They may appear on the screen or be printed on paper. Almost all computer games use graphics, and business, scientific and engineering programs are using more graphics now. This is because drawings and colour can give the computer user more information, more quickly than hundreds of words. The use of graphics in Computer Aided Design (CAD) can help in designing objects from shoes to spacecraft. In some cases, the design computer is also linked to manufacturing machinery: Computer Aided Manufacture (CAM). When a design is agreed, the system can produce samples and finally the finished product. The most powerful computers can produce very lifelike images that are used in television commercials or parts of movies.

▼ *Computers can produce three-dimensional graphics of high quality. This makes them a useful tool for graphic artists.*

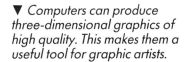

▼ *Engineers use computers in the design of more efficient vehicles. Small changes can be made to the design, and their effects observed, without having to redraw the whole object and make a new model for testing.*

▲ *This effect was achieved by transferring a photograph into a computer animation system and drawing it onto a grid of tiles.*

COMPUTER

The first electronic computer, Colossus, was built in Britain in 1943. It used 1500 electron tubes or valves, each the size of a small bottle and it needed a team of trained operators. The valve was replaced by the transistor in the 1950s. It was a tiny fraction of the size of a valve. Computers became much smaller and the miniaturization has continued ever since. Computers are now built from integrated circuits, or chips, each containing up to several hundred thousand components. The most advanced chip is the microprocessor. It contains a computer's Central Processing Unit (CPU), its control and calculating parts.

Computers affect almost every aspect of our lives. A person travelling on an aircraft has the seat booking made by computer. The aircraft was probably designed and built with the aid of computer-controlled machinery and many of the aircraft's systems are controlled and monitored by computers. Before and during the flight, the crew is supplied with weather reports prepared with the aid of computers.

Many of the letters sent and received every day are prepared on a type of computer called a word processor. If a person has to go to hospital, appointment details and some records are stored on computer files. All sorts of personal and business records are kept on computers.

Computers are also very good at creating lifelike images. Aircraft simulators enable pilots to train without leaving the ground. In a simulator, the detailed scene the pilot sees through the aircraft's windows is created by a computer. The computer's ability to process large amounts of data very quickly is used in scientific research to analyse the results of experiments.

▲ *This computer was used in 1952 to predict the results of the American Presidential election.*

▲ *A modern portable computer.*

▼ *Some of the devices that can be used to input information into a computer are: a joystick, often used when playing games; a mouse for drawing computer graphics; and a keyboard. Disk drives are used for both inputting information and storing it.*

▼ *Computers store data and programs on RAM and ROM chips. The central processing unit (CPU) is the heart of a computer system. Input devices such as a keyboard, and output devices, such as a visual display unit, and a printer are used to communicate between the computer and the user.*

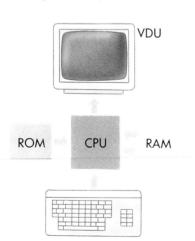

VDU

ROM   CPU   RAM

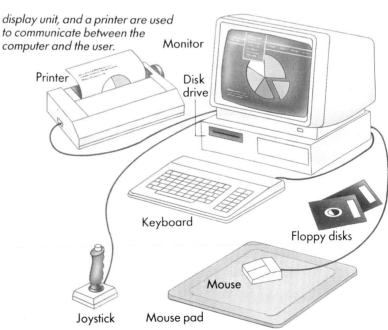

Monitor

Printer

Disk drive

Keyboard

Floppy disks

Mouse

Joystick   Mouse pad

▲ Most home computers can store the rules of computer games and display detailed coloured graphics. Games also have special sound effects to make them more exciting.

▲ A microcomputer can be programmed to enable you to play chess against it. The memory keeps a record of all the moves made.

▲ The resolution of modern computer (and television screens) allows graphics programs to produce very realistic animation.

► Modern, fast and powerful computers still take up quite a lot of space though they are much less bulky than the old-fashioned valve computers. The central processing unit is contained in the upright structures.

▼ A light pen is a device used to input information into a computer. This is done by holding the pen to the screen.

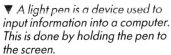

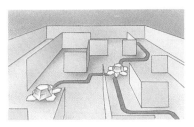

► This mechanical turtle is a robot that moves under computer control. It is used to help teach children about computers; for example, the turtle can be programmed to find its way around a maze (above).

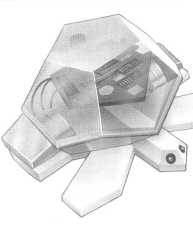

See also HARDWARE; LANGUAGE TRANSLATION BY COMPUTERS; MAGNETIC TAPE; MICROCHIP; MICROPROCESSOR; SOFTWARE.

Program The sequence of instructions given to a computer to make it perform a particular task.

BASIC The initials stand for Beginners' All-purpose Symbolic Instruction Code. This programming language was developed in the 1960s and is one of the most widely used computer languages in the world.

Logo A program language specially designed to allow young children to program using a device called a turtle.

Fortran A program language, first introduced in the 1950s, which is used for scientific work. The name comes from 'formula translation'.

Computer languages

Computer languages enable people to communicate with COMPUTERS. Computers can only process information in the form of a series of NUMBERS. This is practically impossible to understand. A computer language translates the computer operator's instructions into the 'machine code' that the computer uses and translates the computer's coded responses back into words that the human operator can understand.

There are many different computer languages designed to do different work. One of the most popular is BASIC (Beginners' All-purpose Symbolic Instruction Code) because it is easy to learn. Another, Pascal (after the 17th-century French mathematician, Blaise Pascal) was developed as a language for teaching. COBOL (Common Business Oriented Language) is used for writing financial programs. Logo uses simple instructions to control a 'turtle'. The turtle may be a small ROBOT that travels across the floor, connected to the computer by cable, or it may be a drawing on the screen. When the robot moves it draws a line. Logo teaches children how to analyse a problem, write a program to solve it and correct any mistakes, or 'bugs', in it.

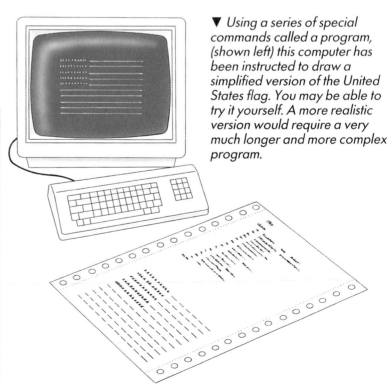

▼ Using a series of special commands called a program, (shown left) this computer has been instructed to draw a simplified version of the United States flag. You may be able to try it yourself. A more realistic version would require a very much longer and more complex program.

A BASIC program
```
LIST
5 FOR ROW = 1 TO 5
10 FOR STAR = 1 TO 10
15 PRINT "*";
20 NEXT STAR
25 FOR STRIPE = 1 TO 20
30 PRINT "=";
35 NEXT STRIPE
40 PRINT
45 NEXT ROW
50 FOR ROW = 1 TO 5
55 FOR STRIPE = 1 TO 30
60 PRINT "=";
65 NEXT STRIPE
70 PRINT
75 NEXT ROW
RUN
```

Computer memory

Computer memory is like a set of pigeon holes. Each has an address. The address is a number that identifies it. Here it can store one unit of information. The COMPUTER is made up of various INTEGRATED CIRCUITS, or chips. Some form the computer's memory. Other chips control how information flows into and out of the computer.

There are two types of memory, Read Only Memory (ROM) and Random Access Memory (RAM). ROM stores programs that tell the computer how to process data and control its various parts. RAM is a temporary data store. Data in RAM is lost when the computer is switched off. The memory is connected to the computer's Central Processing Unit (CPU) by a data bus, an address bus, a read line and a write line. A bus is a connection with several paths or wires so that several signals can be sent along it at the same time.

To store data, the CPU sends a signal along the write line to tell the memory that it wants to store (or write) data. It then sends the address where the data is to be stored on the address bus. The CPU sends the data on the data bus to the memory, where it is stored as electrical charges. To obtain data from (or read) the memory, the CPU sends a signal on the read line and then the address on the address bus. A copy of the contents of the address is sent to the CPU.

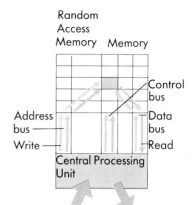

▲ Computers connect their three parts with links called buses down which data can be passed. Two types of computer memory are shown, RAM and ROM. Information can be put in or taken out of the RAM memory. The ROM memory has the computer's operating instructions on it and can't be changed.

Concentration

The concentration of a substance is the amount of that substance that exists in relation to something else. For example salt dissolves in water and the more salt you add the more salty the water will be. The salt is the SOLUTE, water the SOLVENT. The more solute there is dissolved

SEE FOR YOURSELF
Mix 10 heaped teaspoons of salt into half a glass of water. Add some colouring to your salt solution. Carefully pour half a glass of fresh water on top. Gently lower an egg into the glass. It floats in the middle at the surface of the salt solution, which is more dense than the fresh water above it.

Removing waste from metal ores is called concentrating the ore. Lead ore, for example, is crushed into particles and mixed with water and oily chemicals. The concentrate floats to the surface and is skimmed off. With further treatment the lead becomes purer and purer until concentrations of 99.9999 percent lead are sometimes achieved.

SEE FOR YOURSELF
The steam from a boiling kettle escapes from the hot water inside into the colder air outside and forms water vapour. Put on a glove and hold a spoon in the steam. Tiny drops of water condense from the vapour and form on the spoon. These collect together and fall off the spoon as larger water drops.

in the solvent, the higher the concentration of the solution. The concentration of a solute in a solvent is at its highest when the solution is SATURATED. The concentration of a solution is usually expressed as a percentage and indicates how many units of solute are dissolved in 100 units of solvent. The higher the concentration of a substance the greater the number of MOLECULES of that substance in a particular volume.

See also DIFFUSION; OSMOSIS.

Concrete *See* Cement

Condensation

Condensation is the process by which a GAS or a VAPOUR forms a LIQUID when it is cooled. The cooling causes the gas molecules to slow down, so the forces of attraction between them make them stick more closely together. As they become closer together they become a liquid. For example, water vapour which evaporates during cooking often condenses on the inside of the lid of the saucepan, and some of the water vapour in the air in a room can condense on the cold windows. Mist, fog and CLOUDS are produced when air which contains a lot of water vapour is cooled and the water condenses into very small droplets. If the droplets are large enough they fall to the ground as rain. Condensation is important in industry for purifying substances, and in DISTILLATION, where a liquid is condensed and collected.

See also BOILING POINT; PRECIPITATION.

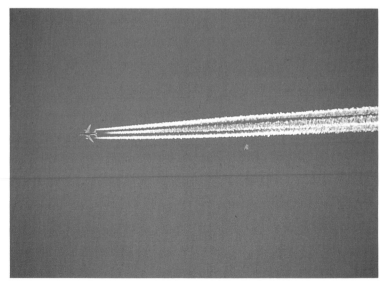

▶ *Contrails, sometimes seen in the sky behind aircraft, consist of tiny water droplets. Water vapour from the exhaust of the aircraft's engines condenses in the cold air. Contrail is an abbreviation of condensation trail.*

Condenser *See Capacitor*

Conduction, heat

Heat conduction (or thermal conduction) is the process by which HEAT travels through a material. This happens in all materials because MOLECULES in the hotter parts vibrate more quickly than molecules in the colder parts; the molecules that move more quickly bump into the more slowly moving ones and transfer ENERGY to them. This means that heat tends to travel through the material or substance from the hot parts to the colder parts. The best conductors of heat are METALS, since the ELECTRONS which carry electric current can also carry energy from hot parts to cold parts. Gases are by comparison poor

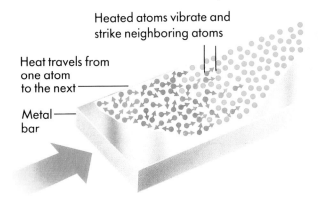

Heated atoms vibrate and strike neighboring atoms

Heat travels from one atom to the next

Metal bar

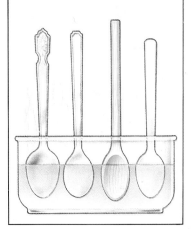

◀ *Heat flows from the hot part of an object to the cold part. The rapidly moving atoms in the hot part strike the less energetic atoms in the cold part and speed them up.*

conductors, since the molecules which make them up are relatively far apart and do not collide very often. In a gas or a liquid, CONVECTION, which involves heat being carried by the circulation of the fluid, tends to carry more heat than conduction unless prevented from doing so by restricting movement of the fluid. Heat can also be transferred by RADIATION, which does not require any material to travel through.

See also INSULATION, THERMAL; THERMODYNAMICS.

▼ *Current moves through materials that conduct electricity. Copper makes one of the best conductors and so is used to make wires and electrical connections. This diagram shows a section through a wire.*

Conductors, electric

Electric conductors are MATERIALS that can carry an electric current. The best conductors are METALS, because in these the ELECTRONS can move freely through the material, carrying the current. As the electrons move, they strike the ATOMS and make them vibrate; this interferes

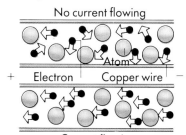

No current flowing

Atom

+ Electron   Copper wire −

Current flowing

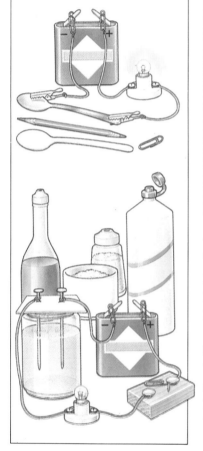

Gustav R. Kirchhoff (1824–1887)
Kirchhoff was a German physicist. In 1845, he worked out a set of laws called Kirchhoff's laws. These laws made it possible to work out the amount of current flowing at any point in a network of electric conductors. He also showed that alternating current in an electric conductor with no resistance travels at the speed of light. With the German chemist Robert Bunsen he developed the modern spectroscope. They used the spectroscope and a prism specially designed by Kirchhoff to analyse substances. In 1860, they showed that when metal compounds are heated in a flame, each gives off a spectrum particular to the metal. It was by using this technique that Kirchhoff and Bunsen discovered the elements caesium and rubidium.

From laws he developed about the emission and absorption of radiation, he suggested the concept of the black body. This was a key step in the development of the branch of physics known as quantum mechanics.

with the current flow and causes the material to heat up. This is electrical RESISTANCE. Good conductors have low resistance. Nowadays the best conductors are not familiar metals like COPPER, but are synthetic materials made from HYDROCARBONS.

Materials in which the electrons are not free to move separately are known as INSULATORS. Electrical conduction in solid insulators involves the movement of whole atoms and is much more difficult. There is also a class of materials, known as SEMICONDUCTORS, in which the electrons are almost, but not quite, free to move.

Conservation

A quantity is said to be conserved if, no matter how complicated the system, it does not change. For example, in CHEMICAL REACTIONS the total number of ATOMS of every ELEMENT is conserved; when hydrogen is burned in oxygen to form water, there are just as many hydrogen and oxygen atoms in the water at the end as there were in the starting materials.

It used to be thought that, since all substances are made up of atoms, the total amount of MASS present would also be conserved. However, the theory of RELATIVITY tells us that mass is a form of ENERGY and that it can be converted into other forms, for example, heat. It is the total energy, not just mass, which is conserved. This effect is too small to be measured in chemical reactions, but is important to NUCLEAR ENERGY.

Conservation, environmental

Conservation is the management of the ENVIRONMENT, in all aspects, in such a way that its quality and natural RESOURCES are maintained. It does not necessarily mean that particular forms of wildlife, habitats or climates, for example, should be protected and preserved unchanging for ever. Conservation recognizes that any natural system is constantly changing. Although humans evolved as part of the Earth's natural environment, our activities are often very damaging on a large scale. It is, therefore, necessary for humans to manage the environment, and the effects they have upon it, wisely. This means, for example, that, in world terms, a wide variety of animals and plants should be preserved, that resources, such as MINERALS or ENERGY, should be used sparingly, and that POLLUTION should be reduced.

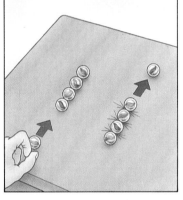

SEE FOR YOURSELF
Place 4 marbles in a row. Take another marble and roll it into the end of the row of marbles. The impact of the marble causes energy to be transferred between the marbles in the line. The marble at the end is propelled forward but the other marbles do not move. Since the energy is conserved, the energy of the moving marble is transferred to the marble at the end of the row and it moves.

People are becoming more aware that we must conserve our environment before it is too late. A number of United Nations agencies coordinate conservation on a worldwide basis. Mediterranean nations have agreed to work together to clean up the water of the sea and prevent oil spills. African and Asian countries are establishing national parks.

◀ *Paper is just one of a number of products that can be recycled and turned into new paper goods. Waste paper is collected and stored as bales before being transported to a mill to be processed. Other products that can be recycled include aluminium cans and glass.*

▼ *Different constellations can be seen in the skies of the Northern and Southern Hemispheres. The 12 constellations which the Sun passes through in the course of a year are known as the signs of the zodiac.*

Constellation

People usually think of a constellation as a group of stars, such the seven bright stars of Ursa Major (the Great Bear). It is really one of the areas, arbitrarily named by astronomers, that fit together to make up the

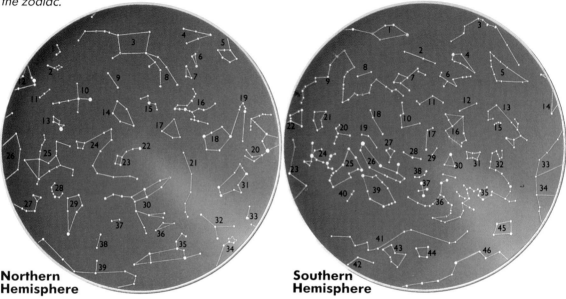

Northern Hemisphere

Southern Hemisphere

Constellations of the Northern Hemisphere	
1 *Equuleus*	29 *Boötes*
2 *Delphinus*	30 *Ursa Major*
3 *Pegasus*	31 *Gemini*
4 *Pisces*	32 *Cancer*
5 *Cetus*	33 *Canis Minor*
6 *Aries*	34 *Hydra*
7 *Triangulum*	35 *Leo*
8 *Andromeda*	36 *Leo Minor*
9 *Lacerta*	37 *Canes Venatici*
10 *Cygnus*	38 *Coma Berenices*
11 *Sagitta*	39 *Virgo*
12 *Aquila*	
13 *Lyra*	
14 *Cepheus*	
15 *Cassiopeia*	
16 *Perseus*	
17 *Camelopardus*	
18 *Auriga*	
19 *Taurus*	
20 *Orion*	
21 *Lynx*	
22 Pole or North star	
23 *Ursa Minor*	
24 *Draco*	
25 *Hercules*	
26 *Ophiuchus*	
27 *Serpens*	
28 *Corona Borealis*	

Constellations of the Southern Hemisphere			
1 *Cetus*	13 *Sagittarius*	25 *Puppis*	36 *Centaurus*
2 *Sculptor*	14 *Aquila*	26 *Carina*	37 *Crux*
3 *Aquarius*	15 *Corona Australis*	27 *Volans*	38 *Musca*
4 *Piscis Austrinus*	16 *Pavo*	28 *Chamaeleon*	39 *Vela*
5 *Capricornus*	17 *Octans*	29 *Apus*	40 *Pyxis*
6 *Grus*	18 *Dorado*	30 *Triangulum Australe*	41 *Hydra*
7 *Phoenix*	19 *Pictor*		42 *Sextans*
8 *Fornax*	20 *Columba*	31 *Ara*	43 *Crater*
9 *Eridanus*	21 *Lepus*	32 *Scorpio*	44 *Corvus*
10 *Hydrus*	22 *Orion*	33 *Serpens*	45 *Libra*
11 *Tucana*	23 *Monoceros*	34 *Ophiuchus*	46 *Virgo*
12 *Indus*	24 *Canis Major*	35 *Lupus*	

sky. Constellations are all different shapes and sizes. Some constellations contain very few bright stars, for example, the largest constellation, Hydra (the Water Snake), is so dim that few people know of it, but everyone has heard of the smallest, Crux (the Southern Cross).

Many of the constellations were named before 2000 BC by Babylonian astronomers. The oldest are the 12 forming the zodiac. By AD 150, when the Greek astronomer Ptolemy published his famous star catalogue, he listed 48. No more were added until explorers began to sail South and saw parts of the sky invisible from Europe and the Mediterranean. The total number is now 88.

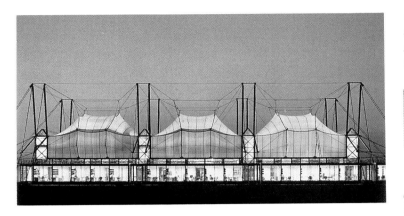

◄ *The building of complicated elaborate structures has been made possible by advances in construction technology.*

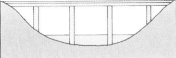

Beam bridge

Cantilever bridge

Arch bridge

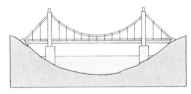

Suspension bridge

▲ *Examples of some of the most common types of bridge design.*

Construction

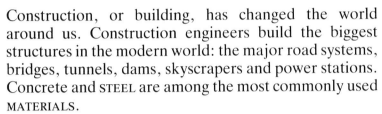

Construction, or building, has changed the world around us. Construction engineers build the biggest structures in the modern world: the major road systems, bridges, tunnels, dams, skyscrapers and power stations. Concrete and STEEL are among the most commonly used MATERIALS.

Every structure has a natural FREQUENCY called its resonant frequency. Any structure that vibrates at its resonant frequency may shake so violently that it tears itself apart. Engineers must be careful that the flow of wind or water around a structure does not cause resonant vibration. Models of proposed structures are tested in WIND TUNNELS to ensure this does not happen. Analysis of structures by COMPUTER helps to predict problems.

Some shapes are particularly strong. Tubes and triangles are the strongest. Steel structures such as bridges and ELECTRICITY pylons are composed of steel struts bolted together to form hundreds of triangles. This is the most efficient way of spreading forces evenly throughout the structure. Tunnels and the legs of oil rigs are often tubular because this shape resists bending.

SEE FOR YOURSELF
Using pipecleaners and straws, experiment with a variety of different constructions. The pipecleaners can be bent to form different joints to join the straws. You could try making the construction illustrated. The criss-cross pattern gives it extra strength. Try using your construction to support a weight.

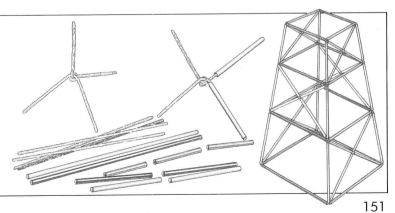

Continent

A continent is any one of the seven main land masses of the world: Europe, Asia, North America, South America, Africa, Australia and Antarctica. The arctic region is not a continent because it consists largely of water, some of which is frozen. Less than one-third of the EARTH's surface area is occupied by the continents; the rest is OCEANS and the smaller areas of land.

The Earth's crust beneath the continents is thicker and more complex than that beneath the oceans. Continental crust is, on average, about 35 km thick although where major MOUNTAIN chains, such as the Himalayas, occur, the crust may be up to 50 km thick. And, whereas oceanic crust is made up of largely basalt-like rocks, the continents are mainly granite overlain by various SEDIMENTARY and METAMORPHIC rocks. Most scientists now believe that the continents are still growing and new continental crust is being formed by remelting oceanic crust. *See also* PLATE TECTONICS.

▼ The major land masses on the Earth's surface are called continents.

▼ Contraction causes electric cables to hang higher in the winter cold than in summer. The cables therefore appear low in the summer.

Contraction

Contraction is the name given to the shrinking or decrease in volume of a substance. This can happen due to the substance becoming colder. As the substance cools, the MOLECULES which make it up vibrate less and the forces of attraction between them are able to bind them together more closely, so the substance shrinks slightly. Contraction also occurs in GASES due to changes in PRESSURE, normally because of increases in pressure.

The ability of materials to expand and contract has to be taken into consideration by the CONSTRUCTION industry when choosing MATERIALS. Unless the design allows for contraction it can produce distortion or cracking in the structure which would make it unsafe. Large road bridges, for example, have EXPANSION joints which are clearly visible.

Convection

Convection is the process in FLUIDS in which, because of changes in DENSITY, the LIQUID or GAS rises or falls. For example, if a liquid is heated the liquid near the HEAT source warms up first and expands. It becomes less dense, therefore, and tends to rise and cold fluid comes in to take its place. The rise of the hot fluid and the fall of the cold fluid transports heat from one place to another. Heat also travels by CONDUCTION and RADIATION, but these do not involve the movement of the material itself as does convection.

Convection is important in heating and insulating homes. Storage heaters and central heating radiators warm a room by producing convection currents which distribute the heated air around. Double glazing windows helps prevent heat from escaping from a room because the narrow space between the two panes of glass is not big enough for convection to develop and transport heat. Convection also occurs in the ATMOSPHERE; rising currents of warm air can allow birds to soar for a very long time without flapping their wings at all.
See also EXPANSION; THERMODYNAMICS.

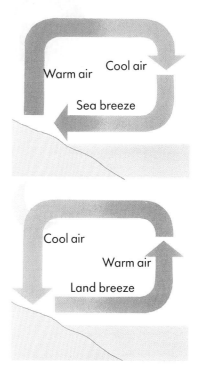

▲ Sea breezes are caused by convection currents. During the day, the land heats up more quickly than the sea. Air over the land becomes warmer and rises. Cooler air from the sea moves in to take its place. At night, the land cools down more quickly than the sea. A convection current is formed in the opposite direction to the daytime current. Warm air over the sea rises and cool air from the land moves in to take its place.

◄ The hang-glider is carried across the sky on a current of air, a convection current.

153

▲ The feat of juggling needs excellent coordination. A continuous flow of information (feedback) is sent to and from the hands and brain.

Coordination

Coordination is the combination of mind and MUSCLES which allows animals to move smoothly and without injury. This happens automatically, once it has been learned as a young animal, for example, a child. A young child cannot coordinate mind and muscles sufficiently to catch a ball, but this skill is learned rapidly.

Each movement we make involves a very complex set of instructions sent from the BRAIN to the muscles, and further signals which are returned to the brain, telling it how far the muscle has moved, and when it has completed the activity. All of this involves millions of electrical signals passing to and from the brain. It also uses REFLEXES, which involve the muscles and a part of the nervous system outside the brain, and so can take place very rapidly. A blink is a reflex, and so is the rapid movement of your finger away from a hot object. Most movement is controlled by automatic coordination. We do not have to think about how to walk, because this skill has been learned and the body coordinates it. All we need to do is to decide where to walk, and how fast to move. If you try to learn a new skill such as gymnastics, you need to practise all over again until the body can coordinate the movements automatically.

See also GLANDS; HORMONE; LEARNING; NERVES.

Copernicus, Nicolaus

Nicolaus Copernicus (1473–1543), a Polish canon or priest, proposed that the SUN and not the EARTH is at the centre of the UNIVERSE. This was dangerous teaching at a time when the Bible was believed to prove that the Earth is the central and most important body of all. Like ARISTARCHUS 1800 years earlier, it made him unpopular.

He published his theory in a book which very few people bought or read, but the fact that it existed was enough to start others discussing the theory. However, proof did not come until the century after Copernicus died. His theory was not completely accurate. First, he believed that the planets move in circles instead of ellipses. Second, he thought that the stars are dim objects not much farther off than the outermost planet then known, Saturn. In other words he thought that the Sun was really at the centre of the Universe instead of being an average star in a huge GALAXY.

▲ Nicolaus Copernicus proposed that the Earth and the planets rotate around the Sun.

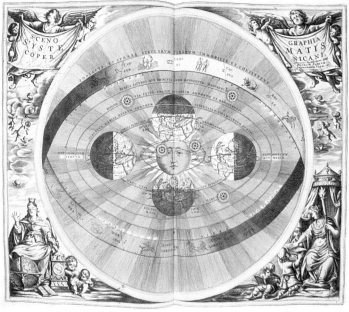

◀ *Copernicus' idea of the Solar System. He thought that the planets went round the Sun in circles. Only later did Kepler show that the orbits are ellipses.*

▼ *The copper ore is crushed to small pieces. Water is mixed with it and it is ground by a ball mill into fine particles to form a slurry. The slurry is heated in a furnace to separate the copper. A converter purifies the molten copper. During the electrolytic refining process an electric current produces chemical reactions, which produce copper metal that is over 99.9 percent pure. The final processing stage consists of melting and casting the copper metal into cakes, billets, bars and ingots.*

Copper

Copper is a soft reddish-brown solid metallic ELEMENT found free in nature and also in copper-bearing minerals in combination with other elements. It may also be found in ores containing lead, zinc, gold, platinum and nickel. Copper has been important to human development since before 3000 BC. Although too soft for most purposes, it can be mixed with other METALS to form very strong ALLOYS, such as brass and bronze. Pure copper is a good CONDUCTOR of ELECTRICITY and is therefore used for electrical wiring. Copper piping is used for plumbing, and copper-nickel alloy is used in coinage. Copper is malleable (can be easily shaped or beaten) and extremely ductile (can be drawn out without breaking). Copper is extracted from its ores and pure copper is refined by ELECTROLYSIS.

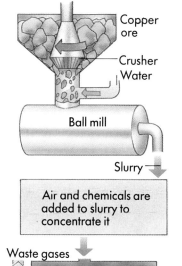

Copper ore

Crusher
Water

Ball mill

Slurry

Air and chemicals are added to slurry to concentrate it

Waste gases

Furnace

Slag

Copper

Cast copper slabs

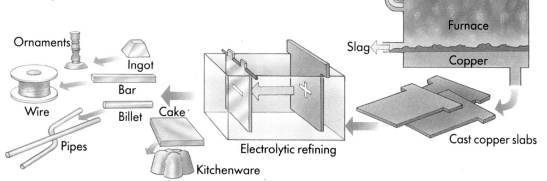

Ornaments

Ingot

Bar

Wire

Billet

Cake

Pipes

Electrolytic refining

Kitchenware

▲ *The Sun's corona cannot normally be seen because of the Sun's brightness. The corona is only visible during an eclipse when the Sun is covered by the Moon.*

Corona

When the Moon passes completely in front of the SUN during an ECLIPSE, a glowing halo shines out. This is the corona, the Sun's atmosphere. The visible part spreads for over 1,000,000 km above the surface, but it continues invisibly further into space. The gas in the corona is thousands of times thinner than our air. Unlike our AT-MOSPHERE, which is held to the Earth by GRAVITY, it is pouring off into space at a speed of about 400 km/s. These clouds of atoms pass the planets and race towards the stars. This movement is the *solar wind*.

Corrosion

Corrosion is the chemical process by which a material such as METAL is tarnished or destroyed by the action of a liquid (usually an ACID, an alkali or water) or a gas (usually oxygen). Rust is a form of corrosion in which iron, exposed to damp air or to water containing impurities, undergoes OXIDATION. The red iron oxide formed is flaky and crumbles away. The surface of an aluminium pan also turns into an oxide, and if scratched or attacked by acid it too can flake away. When an acid or alkali corrodes the surface of a metal, it may eat holes where it reacts with the metal. Oxidation in a dry atmosphere usually causes general tarnishing. Corrosion under moist conditions or when a metal lies under water is caused by ELECTROLYSIS, with one part of the metal forming an anode and another a cathode. Air pollution by gases such as sulphur dioxide and nitrogen dioxide, which produce ACID RAIN, are sources of corrosion. Painting or electroplating metal helps to protect it.

Some metals, such as steel, are often coated with a thin layer of a second metal to improve their resistance to corrosion. This is carried out by the process of electroplating, which is an application of electrolysis. Bathroom taps are coated with chromium and cutlery with silver, nickel or chromium.

SEE FOR YOURSELF
Take 2 iron nails and paint 1 of them. Place both nails in a shallow tray. Put the tray outside. After a few days the unpainted iron nail goes rusty. After a few months rust spots appear through the paint on the painted nail. Rust is the most common form of corrosion; it forms on iron and steel that has been exposed to moist air or water.

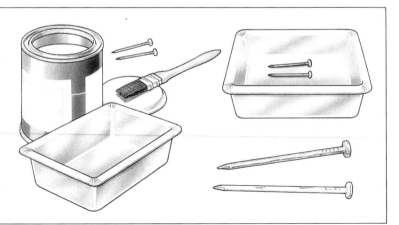